✠

Hymns Today
and Tomorrow

✠
Hymns Today and Tomorrow

ERIK ROUTLEY

Ⓐ *Abingdon Press New York • Nashville*

HYMNS TODAY AND TOMORROW

Copyright © 1964 by Abingdon Press

Library of Congress Catalog Card Number: 64-21135

SET UP, PRINTED, AND BOUND BY THE
PARTHENON PRESS, AT NASHVILLE,
TENNESSEE, UNITED STATES OF AMERICA

Acknowledgments

Grateful acknowledgment is given to the following authors and owners of copyrights for their kind permission to quote from the hymns listed below.

Jonathan Cape, Ltd., and the executors of the Laurence Housman estate for "Father eternal, ruler of Creation," whose first inclusion in a Hymnal was in *Songs of Praise*, 1925.

J. M. Dent & Sons Ltd., for "Of the Father's heart begotten," translated by R. F. Davis, from the Temple Classics series.

H. Emerson Fosdick for "God of grace and God of glory."

Morehouse-Barlow Co., Inc., for "And have the bright immensities" from *The Way of Light,* by Howard C. Robbins; and "I sing a song of the saints of God" from *Everyday Hymns for Children,* by Lesbia Scott.

Oxford University Press for "Wake, O Wake," by F. C. Burkitt; "It is finished," by Gabriel Gillett; "Judge eternal," by H. Scott Holland; and "Son of God, eternal Savior," by S. C. Lowry, all from *The English Hymnal*. For "When a knight won his spurs" and "We thank you, Lord of heaven," by Jan Struther; "Sing my tongue," translated by Percy Dearmer, all from *Songs of Praise*, enlarged edition. For "Jesus, whose all-redeeming love," by G. W. Briggs, from *Hymns of the Faith;* "God, my Father, loving me," by G. W. Briggs,

Abbreviations Used
Throughout the Book

CE   *The Book of Common Praise.* Toronto: Oxford University Press, 1938.

CH   *The Church Hymnary.* Revised Edition. London: Oxford University Press, 1927.

CP   *Congregational Praise.* London: Independent Press, Ltd., 1951.

CS   *Hymnal for Colleges and Schools.* Edited by E. Harold Geer. New Haven: Yale University Press, 1956.

CU   *The Hymnary.* United Church of Canada. Toronto: The United Church Publishing House, 1930.

EH   *The English Hymnal.* London: Oxford University Press, 1933.

H   *The Hymnal.* Protestant Episcopal Church. New York: The Church Pension Fund, 1940.

HAMR   *Hymns Ancient and Modern.* Revised Edition. London: The Proprietors of *Hymns Ancient and Modern,* 1958.

HAMSt   *Hymns Ancient and Modern.* Standard Edition. London: The Proprietors of *Hymns Ancient and Modern,* 1924.

L   *Service Book and Hymnal.* Lutheran. Minneapolis: Ausburg Publishing House, 1958.

M   *The Methodist Hymnal.* Nashville: The Methodist Publishing House, 1935.

MR   Hymn will be in the forthcoming revision of the Methodist Hymnal.

MHB   *The Methodist Hymn-Book.* London: Methodist Conference Office, 1933.

MSHB   *The School Hymn Book of the Methodist Church.* London: Methodist Youth Department, 1950.

OA   *The Oxford American Hymnal for Schools and Colleges.* Edited by C. F. Pfatteicher. London: Oxford University Press, 1930.

P *Pilgrim Hymnal.* Congregational-Christian. Boston: The Pilgrim Press, 1958.

PR *The Hymnbook.* Presbyterian. Philadelphia: John Ribble, 1955.

SP *Songs of Praise.* Enlarged edition. London: Oxford University Press, 1931.

SSP *Sunday School Praise.* London: National Sunday School Union, 1958.

Preface

I hold it a high honor to be invited by so distinguished an American publishing house to write this book. I write as an Englishman, now domiciled in Scotland, who has been on two occasions a guest in the United States, and who has many friends who are American citizens.

It is, of course, presumptuous of me to write what I do here write, because a good deal of what I write is critical of the hymn singing customs of our two countries, and might be taken to be critical of customs in the United States. That cannot be gainsaid. Yet I have felt free to write in this way, and to write thus for an American readership because I am convinced that there are people who wish to see hymn singing advance along the road of wisdom, and that many of these live in the United States.

I have been astonished and humbled (speaking as an Englishman) by the zest, the learning, and the sacrificial enthusiasm with which church music is pursued in America. The enterprise and well-informed energy of our friends there put most of us in Britain to shame. Moreover, when I have had the privilege of meeting such experts in hymnology as James R. Sydnor, Professor Grady Davis of Chicago Lutheran Seminary, Ruth Messenger, Leonard Ellinwood, Austin Lovelace, Professor Paul Ensrud of St. Olaf, Northfield, Minnesota, and the staff of the School of Church Music at Union Theological Seminary, New York, I can be left in no doubt that the background in church music in the United States is friendly toward the development of an informed interest in these matters. My friends in the Hymn Society of America would, I am sure, wish to be associated with this sentiment. They have done much to promote this new interest.

But the time has surely come when we should examine our hymn singing at a slightly different level from that at which it is examined in so many good books already existing in the United States. I felt that I could add nothing to the mass of musical exhortation that is now being so well given, and to the weight of information that is being so industriously provided. You have Leonard Ellinwood and Armin Haeussler, and the great work of the late Professor Archibald Davison; and you have excellent works like *The Hymnal* (*1940*) *Companion*. In America you lead the way in hymnological research and teaching.

What I thought I could contribute, however, were some questions about the use of hymns in worship, and especially some incentives to investigation of the *words* of the hymns we sing. This could have made a very large book. I am content here with offering a few examples illustrative of an argument, in the hope that once the examples have been observed, others will occur to the reader; and that once the principle of intelligent criticism is established, the reader will be able to do it better than I can.

So this is not a history of hymns. I do not undertake to mention a large number of hymns. I mention only those which seem to illustrate my contentions. Most of those I mention will be found in American hymnals. But some I have deliberately taken from sources less accessible in the United States, because I thought that the addition of these would add fresh colors to the picture and interest the reader.

If I had written this primarily for a British readership, I should not have written it very differently. It is just possible that in Britain we have made some progress along this particular line (the critical investigation of words, images, and language generally in hymns) — more than has been achieved in the United States. This is probably because where hymns flourish most in Britain (that is, in the Dissenting churches) music has only very recently come to hold a place of honor, and English Dissent is musically far behind the sophistication and skill of churches of the corresponding denominations in the United States. But my conviction is that if this kind of criticism (not necessarily these specific criticisms) were applied generally in the United States, then hymnody there would lead the world.

It is now a matter of "singing praises with understanding." We are all in danger of being sentimental and unreal in worship. I have been unable to conceal my conviction that this danger is often an imminent one—even that in some places the point of no return has been passed. But in the hope that what I write could be in the end constructive, I have been bold enough to set down some ideas on how a hymnal might be edited in an unusual way, and on how the hymns of the future may come to be written. Where I criticize, I may be unjust; where I try to be constructive, I may be fantastic. But if anybody reads this and says to himself, "No, that is not the way to do it, but it has helped me to see what is the right way," then I shall not have written in vain.

ERIK ROUTLEY
Edinburgh
February, 1963

Contents

Introduction
On the Curious Habit of Hymn Singing

Hymn singing is a pleasurable Christian activity especially associated with Protestant worship. And there, for a very large number of Christian Protestants, it begins and ends. The pleasure associated with hymn singing is the pleasure of singing together a familiar song—which means a well-known piece of music. For many people this pleasure is rudely withdrawn if what they are invited to sing is something they do not know very well already. For some the pleasure disappears if the music is not music which they like; and a hymn can be familiar and still disagreeable to its singer. But for the vast majority of singers—it would hardly be unfair to put it at 90 per cent—the pleasure of singing hymns is bound up with their music. I am far from sure than even 10 per cent of singers derive their major pleasure in hymn singing from the words they sing.

That is what this book is about. It is not about the music of hymns, but about their words. It is not a history, but a critical account designed to draw attention to the pleasures that the words of hymns can bring, and to the traps that the words of some hymns can lay for the unwary. It will be part of my purpose to show to what an extent hymn singing at present is a degenerate and even damaging activity; and how far this degeneracy and damage can be replaced by creativeness and profit, if we allow ourselves to be critical and to enjoy our use of hymns.

It will be necessary to say something first about the way in which a hymn conveys its message and fulfills its writer's purpose and the church's purpose; and then we must say something about the way in which hymns ought to be used, and the ways in which they are frequently abused, in public worship.

A hymn, basically, is an opportunity for a congregation to declare its experience and to rejoice in Christian doctrine corporately. A hymn uses music in order to achieve this corporateness; but the words take a logical priority over the music. True, occasionally a hymn is written to carry a tune because somebody wants to get that tune sung. But this is exceptional. And in any case, while a congregation could—and frequently does—engage in corporate speech without music, it does not, in the Western tradition at any rate, engage in corporate music without words.

A hymn, then, uses words in order to help a congregation speak its mind corporately, and music in order to enhance that corporateness. Music is a very primitive means of corporate rejoicing; and its melody and rhythm add a good deal to the activity of corporate speech, making the activity more attractive and more decisive. Actually, very few congregations can speak well in unison, but many can sing very well together.

If a hymn uses words, it follows that it uses reason. But since a hymn is metrical, it also follows that it uses to some extent the artifices of poetry. The relation between hymnody and poetry is never easy to trace. It is well known that very few poets who were masters of their craft have been successful hymn writers, or indeed attempted hymn writing at all. Only William Cowper and Robert Bridges in the English tradition were both great poets and considerable writers of hymns. Far more great musicians have enriched the repertory of tunes; great poets have not been great hymn writers. This in itself is not difficult to explain. Writing hymns means writing words such as can be sung to a tolerably simple tune by a crowd. This imposes on the writer a discipline which most large-scale poets would find frustrating; short verses, a very decided meter without metrical exchanges or added syllables, and usually rhyme are required. Irregular lines, long stanzas, wayward meters are useless in hymns. The consequence is that if you read a hymn aloud, it very nearly always sounds like doggerel. The essence of poetry is flexibility of stress, variation in paragraph length, and all the other subtleties that can run in counterpoint with the poetic discipline. Try singing such a line as

> Of Man's first disobedience, and the fruit
> Of that forbidden tree, . . .

to a line and a half of a typical hymn tune in tens, and it will be immediately evident that writing blank verse is one thing, and writing a good hymn, another. On the other hand, try reading a really good hymn as poetry—even "When I survey the wondrous Cross" —and the uniformity of stress and stanza length becomes intolerable to the ear, however hallowed the words to the religious consciousness.

Hymn writing, then, is poetry under strict discipline. But more— hymn writing is lyric under a vow of renunciation. It is more like writing opera than writing a song. Sir Donald Tovey once pointed out how a good opera libretto virtually is bound to read like something thin and feeble when it is divorced from its music. Were it too profound and pregnant in its own right, the music might sound like a needless addition. Music cannot carry words when they are the work of a poet in full flight, unless that music is itself very free and subtle.

It may well be noted that during the twentieth century musicians have shown themselves far more ambitious in their choice of words for their songs than they used to be. Sir Hubert Parry was one of the first to aim high, in his "Songs of Farewell" (1917), where at one point he sets to incomparable music a poem of John Donne; he had already, many years before, written an equally immortal setting of Milton's "Blest Pair of Sirens." And Benjamin Britten, to name but one other of a new generation, has carried all this much further. Yet it still remains true that the mightiest gestures of the poet are self-sufficient, and that a musical intrusion, except the music be exceedingly modest, is thought of as unwarrantable.

It is much worse with hymns because they must be "popular" in a sense in which "popularity" is not required in a continuous work like Parry's "Blest Pair of Sirens." The music of the conventional hymn is based on the eighteenth-century dance forms—the Minuet and the *bourrée* are the most obvious. Strict and invariable three-time or four-time, with emphasis at the beginning of the bar, and, as often as not, an eight-bar pattern, are the norm. To write fine poetry within so restricted a framework is a task which the great poet, especially one of romantic or epic aspirations, finds too hard for him. He may write a sonnet; but what he cannot write, except he be a person of very unusual gifts, is a brief lyrical ballad of about twenty lines without metrical variation.

This is not the place to comment on this, or to answer the question whether or not it is an unfair restriction. Whether a future age will demand, and get, hymns of a freer kind, which allowing greater freedom to the writer will proportionately increase the demands on the singer, is an open question. I shall not here deal with it. I am concerned with the situation we find ourselves in at present.

And that situation is made more intriguing, and more perilous, by the fact that while all that we have said about the poet's restrictions when he is writing a hymn is surely true and obvious, yet it remains that very few hymn writers can avoid writing some sort of poetry when they are at their work. For even if you are writing only half a dozen stanzas of common meter, the very conventionality and artificiality of the mode you are writing in makes it necessary for you to write compactly, to say less than you mean, to suggest ideas by images, and to use language that will fit in with the conventions of rhyme. Not every poet is a hymn writer; but every hymn writer is a kind of poet, and what I am going to discuss here is primarily the very odd consequences of forcing a poetic gift through a narrow and oddly shaped channel.

Now the hymn writer cannot do his work effectively unless he has a clear idea of how his work is going to be used. What precisely is his purpose? Why write hymns at all?

His completed work needs to be a combination of doctrine and experience. What he *says* needs to be based on doctrine. He is writing about God, or about God's works. He is also writing about the church's experience of God—about the forgiveness of sins or the communion of saints or the duty of man in society as in the sight of God. What he writes is not a hymn if it is simply about mankind. True, some poems of a humanist sort have almost become hymns because of their common use in church services. But—not to anticipate a line of criticism which has its proper place a little later in our argument—let us be as broad as we can here, and say that a hymn needs at least to have something about it of the supernatural, the aspiring, the upward reach. This will, for the present, allow such a lyric as "City of God" to be a hymn. And in a very real sense it is a hymn, although it contains in itself a minimum of doctrine, and the God whom it mentions could be the patronal deity of any religious or pseudo-religious organization. But basically its writer, a religious man, meant it to be a hymn, and it has had enormous success among congregations because it produces a certain very clear effect. It induces thoughts about the church which its author held with conviction, and it impresses those thoughts on the singer's mind through the adroit use of imaginative language. The watch fires, the shining towers, the unavailing assault of the angry surge are devices of poetry invoked in order that the singer may hear more than the literal words that he is singing. Moreover, when a man sings "City of God," he says not only, "Samuel Johnson thinks that, and I agree," but, quite simply, "I think that"; and when a congregation sings it, they are not far from saying, "We think this. This is our own idea." A fine tune and well-written words are not only attractive, they are persuasive. And that is where the controversy that I am here interested in begins. The writer uses poetry as much as he can; the musician adds music (or, as in this particular case, an inspired editor weds the words and music and others copy him), and the result is something that goes right into the heart of the congregation, and comes out not as Samuel Johnson being sung by a group of Christians, but as a group of Christians stating its belief. Had Samuel Johnson set down in prose what he means in "City of God" a man might read him, or a congregation might hear him read, and say, "That is Johnson's view. I am interested." But because it is poetry, and more because it is a skillfully constructed congregational hymn, a person may sing it and say, "This is my view. I have always thought this."

I said earlier that a hymn writer uses reason as well as poetry. This is important. Should he at any point outrage reason, this will not be noticed by any but the most discerning singers while the hymn is being sung. Therefore an unreasonable notion, a nonsense, will be injected into the congregation, and appear as that congregation's accepted doctrine. If the poet lies, the lie will similarly appear. If the poet uses an image that is not fully understood, or that

21

has changed its terms of relevance with the passing of time, the congregation will accept it at its face value and repeat it, and very probably be deceiving itself.

It would be too much to say that congregations remember their hymns. A few hymns remain wholly in the mind of every instructed Christian, and these are often those which he learned early. On the whole, memories are too short, however, to make it possible to argue from this ground. But nonetheless, a congregation's general temper, its disposition toward right belief or away from it, is subtly influenced by the habitual use of hymns. Therefore it is right to call for caution in their use and choice, because there is no single influence in public worship that can so surely condition a congregation to self-deception, to fugitive follies, to religious perversities, as thoughtlessly chosen hymns. The singing congregation is uncritical: to argue that because it is uncritical what it sings matters not is a disastrous fallacy.

In the following chapters I am going to make one further assumption. These seem to be days in which we shall serve the church best if we are critical, rather than if we allow too much benefit of doubt. The cultural revolution of our time requires that our faith be stated in terms which do not suggest a flight from that revolution. It particularly requires that Christians shall not appear to be people who wish they lived a hundred years ago, and who are temperamentally opposed to this cultural revolution. On the whole, even where we are hospitable to the new criticisms of our dogmas and expressions of faith which the new age brings, in hymns we are slothfully conservative. We may *argue* like people who expect the Word of God to be new every morning, but we do not normally *sound* like such people when we sing hymns. Therefore, I am going to subject some of the assumptions of our hymns and hymn singing to a scrutiny which will often appear overprecise. It may well be that there is more room for liberality than I am here going to allow; but in the correction of my errors, wiser and more humane minds will, I think, provide enlightenment for our singers, and the right road may eventually be found.

1. The
Deception of Images

The Cultural Revolution of Our Time

Three components of what I have called the cultural revolution of our time seem to me to be especially relevant to this criticism.

In the first place, there is biblical criticism. It may seem late in the day to mention this as part of a revolution, but the fact is that the hymn writers have not shown much sign of noticing it. What hymn writers and singers need to decide is what effect, for example, Rudolf Bultmann's theory of demythologization ought to have on our hymn writing, and what effect on our use of hymns is likely to be made by the increasing usage of modern translations of the Scriptures which remove the familiar images and turns of phrase from the worshiper's familiarity. In what sense are many of our hymns naïvely fundamentalist?

In the second place, there is the scientific criticism of accepted Christian methods of thought. Here I do not mean the kind of scientific criticism of biblical mythology that would come under my first head—all the by-now ancient controversies about whether Genesis 1 is or is not an outrage to a modern mind. I mean, rather, the encounter between modern scientific method, which bases itself on the study of evidences and collation of experiments and entirely refuses to erect dogmas in advance of proved truths, and the dogmatic and revelational method of Christianity. This is a matter of vital importance. Christians express, sometimes crudely, sometimes subtly,

23

a crass philistinism toward science and its methods; and few in the "rank and file" have caught up with the proposition boldly made by John Wren-Lewis, a young English scientist, that modern science is the most Christian thing that has happened to the world since the primitive ages of the church. What this complete revolution in method and culture has to do with hymn singing may well be a matter for wonder; but I believe, and shall try to show, that it is central to the whole scheme.

The third factor is closely associated with the second. It is the encounter which Englishmen now know as the controversy of the two cultures, whose key figure is Sir Charles Snow. Here the proposition is that the old classical culture of the eighteenth- and nineteenth-century gentleman has been replaced, or must be replaced, by a new scientific culture; and to men of classical mind this sounds frightening. The relevance of this controversy here is that it gives prominence to a new attitude toward literature which is growing up in our time. Since hymns are literature and use the means of communication that are open to imaginative writers, their impact on a public of the new culture may have to be closely examined.

How Hymn Writers Use Images

With these matters in mind, let us consider in the first place the way in which hymn writers use images to impress upon the singer, and evoke from him, truths of Christian experience. We can divide literary conceits in hymnody into the following categories:

1. Images taken from the Scriptures directly. Of these there is an enormous number. Most are wholly acceptable, some are questionable, many are an illumination and an adornment.

2. Turns of phrase taken from the King James Version of the Scriptures. This is a different matter, being a matter not of images but of vocabulary and syntax. Not infrequently it raises the question of whether or not the singer is familiar enough with the King James Version to pick up the allusion or be pleased by the reminiscence.

3. Images taken from nonscriptural sources such as church custom or secular life. The most obvious of these is the image of snow at Christmas.

4. Purely poetic conceits, which are mostly to be found in hymns that are adaptations of the work of poets who did not think of them-

selves as hymn writers. George Herbert is a very eminent example.

5. Devices of the versifier, which are technical and conventional, and which not infrequently throw an indifferent lyricist into bathos.

Many hymns are, of course, more or less faithful paraphrases of extended passages of scripture. Of these the most faithful are the metrical psalms of England and Scotland, the Scottish paraphrases of 1745 and 1781, and the few psalm versions of John Milton of which the best known is "Let us, with a gladsome mind." In these the impact depends on the extent to which the singer is pleasurably reminded of the passage in question. Some psalm versions and scripture paraphrases are fairly free; and not infrequently in Charles Wesley we have what amounts to a versified commentary on a scripture text. The most famous of these is "Come, O thou Traveller." In all such hymns the imagery is dependent on Scripture. On the other hand, many hymns are translations into English from foreign originals. Here the imagery may be forced or dulled through translation, and experience has shown that on the whole translations make far less impact on the singer's imagination than do original hymns, except where the translator has quite unusual gifts, as Catherine Winkworth had, or where the translator permits his imagination, as did Robert Bridges, to roam far from the literal meaning of the original. Paraphrases such as those of Bridges are frequently more effective hymns than exact translations such as those of John Chandler or Edward Caswall. To scholarly minds this fact is disagreeable, but one has only to compare Miss Winkworth's translation of "Christe du beistand," which is not one of her best, with Pusey's "Lord of our life and God of our salvation" (H. 395) to see how a paraphrase, though it may contain much that is irrelevant to the original, can make an impact in a manner hidden from the faithful translator.

Images Taken from Scripture
Father

It will be quite impossible to examine all the scriptural images of which hymn writers have made use. All we can do is to say enough to arouse the reader's critical interest, and perhaps to direct him to some of the felicities which a true appreciation of the matter will bring.

We may well begin by considering some of the ways in which a certain basic image of God has been used in hymns. The Apostles' Creed is not a classic source for imaginative writing, but in its very first sentence it contains a powerful and familiar image, "I believe in God, the Father Almighty." Now "Father," used of God, is a New Testament image rather than an Old Testament one. In this it is an exception to the general rule, for there is far more poetry in the Old Testament than in the New. "Father," however, comes directly from the teachings of Jesus, from his pattern of prayer, and from his addresses to God as "Father."

But at once we must notice that in the Creed the word "Father" is not only an image of God's relation with man but also, and more, an image of God's relation with Jesus Christ. It takes on, in those ages when doctrine was hammered out in terms of philosophy, a metaphysical sense. When we say "Our Father" we are saying something quite different from what we say when we say "his Son, Jesus Christ our Lord."

It is this creedal, metaphysical sense which we overhear in Prudentius' great hymn (about A.D. 400), *"Corde natus ex parentis"*— "Of the Father's heart begotten" (EH. 613). And again in Charles Wesley's "Father of Jesus Christ my Lord" (CP. 475). On the whole, we find that authors of the pre-Victorian ages were disposed to use "Father" in this sense rather than in the more intimate sense of "fatherhood" that the Lord's Prayer conveys. There we are saying nothing metaphysical. We are expressing faith in God as protector and as our supreme authority. A very good biblical image in this sense, straight from Luke 11:13, is to be found in Frederick W. Faber's hymn, "My God, how wonderful thou art":

> No earthly father loves like Thee;
> No mother, e'er so mild,
> Bears and forbears, as Thou hast done
> With me, Thy sinful child (CU. 18, st. 6)

This is excellently contrived to recall the parable that explains how much more our Father in heaven loves us than an earthly father loves his child. Yet later in the same hymn Faber goes back to the classical sense: "Father of Jesus, love's reward" (CU. 18, st. 7).

In other hymns of the nineteenth century the word is used more casually, and equally intimately:

> Father of Heav'n, Whose love profound
> A ransom for our souls hath found (HAMSt. 164).

> Eternal Father, strong to save (H. 512).

> Father, hear the prayer we offer (P. 368).

And it is here that the critical mind wants to ask a question. In the New Testament, "Father" is an intimate word but not a sentimental one. Still more so is it in the Old Testament. "Father" is the author of protection and the lawgiver. "Father Almighty" is not a contradiction in terms. But as soon as a sentimental overtone gathers over the word "Father," the question arises whether it is a felicitous image of God at all. For the earthly father is at best a fallible creature. He may be, in the experience of some singer, a brutal, stupid, and unfaithful person. Such a person will not readily associate the idea of fatherhood with wisdom and justice.

Were there not unwise and wicked fathers, then, in those earlier days? Is this a fresh phenomenon? Not at all: sin makes progress in ingenuity, but there is nothing new about it. What does make the modern situation different from that in which our Lord used "Father," or in which Charles Wesley wrote it, is that father as provider, and father as lawgiver, has abdicated. This is familiar to sociologists. Moreover, a psychological consequence of the widespread mental anxiety thus created is an alarming increase in the anxiety of infantilism. There is a tendency to run to father, or to mother, for protection and solace, made the more acute by the fear that father may not be there, and in its acuteness transferred to a father-figure, or, without much difficulty, to a mother-figure. That this is characteristic of our modern society, with its desperately bosom-conscious diffidence, punctuated by alarming gestures of aggressiveness, is beyond question. That we have become singularly maladroit in our management of those family relations which in former days were taken for granted is equally evident. All of this corrupts the image of "Father," and while it does not alter our judgment of the value of hymns containing the image, it must make us aware of the necessity of somehow seeing that it is the true image and not the corrupt one that is in the worshiper's mind, and that he is not encouraged by it to follow any of the deviations which spring from the degeneracy of modern fatherhood.

That is an example of the way in which a familiar, and as one would have thought a blameless, image can subtly turn us away from the right track.

Shepherd

Another example, this time from both Old and New Testaments, is that of the "Shepherd." This picture is usually associated with the twenty-third Psalm, although John 10 is equally a source for thoughts based on it. "The Good Shepherd" is, of course, from John, not from the Psalms.

It is natural that our hymn writers should have allowed their imaginations to range beyond the immediate reference of that most precious of psalms. Isaac Watts introduced a happy conceit, drawn from the parable of the Prodigal Son, in the last verse of one of his versions which begins, "My shepherd will supply my need" (see Appendix B, p. 175):

> There would I find a settled rest
> While others go and come,
> No more a stranger or a guest,
> But like a child at home (CP. 50).

Joseph Addison, in "The Lord my pasture shall prepare," interpreted the psalm in terms of the English countryside, with his "sultry glebe," and "sudden greens and herbage." George Herbert introduced a touch from the Song of Solomon 2:16; 6:3 in his first verse:

> The God of love my Shepherd is,
> And he that doth me feed;
> While he is mine and I am his,
> What can I lack or need? (EH. 93.)

And the ingenious Henry W. Baker, in what became the most famous of all versions apart from the rugged Scottish version ("The

28

Lord's my Shepherd") conflates several other thoughts with that of the psalmist. He begins by lifting George Herbert's third line bodily:

> The King of love my Shepherd is,
>   Whose goodness faileth never (*cf.* Ps. 136);
> I nothing lack while I am his,
>   And he is mine for ever (H. 345).

He goes on to bring in Matt. 18:12, and, later, certain images from the eucharistic customs of the English parish church. Where the psalmist mentions "my enemies" Baker writes:

> Thou spread'st a table in my sight;
>   Thy unction grace bestoweth;
> And O, what transport of delight
> From thy pure chalice floweth!

In passing it may be noted that this hymn is full of versifier's devices (category 5 above) which blur rather than advance the sense. "For ever" in his first verse in tautologous, inserted merely to fill up the rhyme. "Thy unction grace bestoweth" is an awkward phrase (as a child I always thought *unction* must be an adjective and *bestoweth* an intransitive verb), and what is the force of pure in "pure chalice"? This is quite the worst available version of the psalm.

But even so, the images it does arouse in the mind are legitimate. It is characteristic of nineteenth-century England that it should be a "tender shepherd" rather than a "tough shepherd" who takes the center of the picture.

> Loving shepherd of thy sheep,
> Keep thy lamb, in safety keep (EH. 602).

> Jesus is our Shepherd,
>   His the voice we hear;
> Folded in His bosom,
> What have we to fear? (CH. 552.)

> Jesus, tender Shepherd, hear me (H. 241).

In children's hymns this may be tolerable; but unless the singer is quite clear that the lamb is in the shepherd's bosom only because it has wandered and hurt itself, he will soon be thinking that the shepherd is carrying the sheep only to save it the trouble of walking on its own feet. Nothing could be more pernicious than the sickly shepherd pictures that adorn many Sunday school walls. They must come down, and on the whole, hymns which represent the shepherd as an ethereal creature who treats the lambs like babies had better be put aside. The shepherd's business is to go over the moors and collect the stragglers in all weather, and to defend the sheep from wolves.

Rock

Another image from natural experience is that of "the rock," used of God or of Christ. Several experiences meet here. There is, on the one hand the rock, or mountain, as a symbol of high ground upon which the ancients believed religious experience was likely to come more freely than on low ground. The climbing of rocks and mountains still satisfies the lusty ambitions of healthy people today. In the exodus, Moses associated the very presence of God himself with the mountain, while in his distress the psalmist (Ps. 61) prays to be set upon the rock that is higher than himself. On the other hand, Elijah, in the tumult of the storm, hid himself in a cave in the rock (I Kings 19). The New Testament adds a picturesque use of the idea of the rock where our Lord contrasts the fate of the house built on rock with that of the house built on sand. Therefore, in John Newton's fine hymn, "Glorious things of thee are spoken," we sing:

> On the Rock of Ages founded,
> What can shake thy sure repose? (H. 385.)

While on the other hand the same phrase occurs in an even more famous hymn:

> Rock of ages, cleft for me,
> Let me hide myself in thee (H. 471).

Here are two contrasted images using the same word. Romantic stories about the actual composition of "Rock of ages" in a cleft of a Devonian rock are now discounted as fantasy; but it is of all things probable that the author of that hymn knew what it was to shelter under a rock from a rainstorm in the wild Devonshire moors that were his home. The question that must arise is whether it is wise often, or ever, to sing of God as somebody to whom one flies for refuge in life's dangers. The same question arises in an acuter form on singing Charles Wesley's very well-known hymn:

> Jesus, Lover of my soul,
>> Let me to thy bosom fly,
> While the nearer waters roll,
>> While the tempest still is high (H. 415).

Here we come upon another way in which images can slip out of relevance. Without doubt these opening lines of Toplady's and Wesley's were innocent when they were written. (John Wesley did not care for his brother's hymn, but that was because of "lover," not because of "bosom.") Wesley wrote his lines for a specific spiritual condition, and headed them "In Temptation." The gathering waters and the tempest are those of temptation, and they adequately express the condition of, for example, the alcoholic or the nymphomaniac. At a moment of high tension such a phrase as "let me to thy bosom fly" is perhaps tolerable. Unhappily, editors always scorn to print authors' titles, not infrequently with results positively damaging to the sense of their lyrics, and in consequence the ordinary singer thinks he is singing about any kind of external adversity. He is thus persuaded to a very supine and unbiblical sort of religion. Similarly, the tempest from which he is supposed to be hiding in "Rock of ages" is the distraction of a sinful world which tempts him to believe that he can manage without God's grace. Augustus M. Toplady, that fanatical Calvinist, wrote his hymn after a satirical and, to our modern eyes, quite preposterous article which clearly showed his pathological obsession with sin. When you have gone through the article you are, as it were, softened up enough to see what "Rock of ages" is driving at. But to hear either of these hymns sung heartily, or sentimentally, or—as the editors of some hymnbooks suggest in their musical rubrics—"devotionally," by people who are, collectively, about as far from any such experience

31

of sin and temptation as they could be, is to hear a strange and hypocritical profanity.

A Digression on the Interlining of Words

I wish here to interrupt my argument in order to express an opinion which cannot, I think, be agreeable to the minds of American editors, but which nonetheless I hold firmly. I have said that editors do not print titles such as would give a clue to the real meaning of "Jesus, Lover of my soul." English editors are inexcusable in this; but the hands of American editors are tied, because it is the convention there to print one or more stanzas of a hymn between the music staves. Where then could such a title relevantly be placed? But the harm that this practice does in making it impossible to read hymns as literature far outweighs, as I believe, the trifling convenience of those who wish to sing in harmony. It is not too much to say that this practice makes the intelligent singing of hymns— which I distinguish from the smooth, hearty, or easy singing of hymns —almost impossible.

Spirit

Few among Christian doctrines have been so sadly emasculated by a false use of images as that of the Holy Spirit. Here we are in considerable perplexity. Broadly speaking, there are three images which are applied commonly to the work of the Holy Spirit: wind and fire (from Acts 2) and the dove (from Mark 1:10). It is instructive to see into what deep waters a godly and biblical writer of the early nineteenth century, John Keble, could get when he tried to adapt typology to his purpose. His hymn "When God of old came down from heaven" is one of the best examples in the literature of a well-meaning but thoroughly misleading piece of teaching.

> When God of old came down from heaven,
> In power and wrath he came;
> Before his feet the clouds were riven,
> Half darkness and half flame.
>
> [Here a verse is omitted]
>
> But when he came the second time,
> He came in power and love;

Softer than gale at morning prime
Hovered his holy Dove (EH. 158).

The first verse refers to the giving of the law on Mount Sinai, in terms wholly appropriate to the book of Exodus. The second verse (his third, after an elaboration of the opening scene) refers to the baptism of Jesus. Now in the first place, it is doubtful whether the giving of the law is rightly represented as a coming of the Holy Spirit. To ancient Israel it was more than that—the self-revelation of God himself. The "spirit" in the Old Testament is an intermittent visitation such as inspires the prophet in ecstasy, gives creative energy to a musician, or gives great strength to such a superman as Samson. The spirit can, of course, be an evil spirit as well as a God-sent one. To link Sinai with Pentecost is false exegesis. But what then happens is much worse, because although in the matter of wind and fire Sinai does at least look like Pentecost, and clearly this is why Keble started where he did, what he next refers to is the baptism of Jesus: and this brings in the dove.

Now the dove is, at one point in the teaching of Jesus, the symbol of innocence and gentleness (Matt. 10:16, "Be . . . harmless as doves"); but to interpret the dove of Mark 1:10 in this way is to make nonsense of the picture. What is this silly bird doing, when people are hearing the voice of God and it sounds like thunder? The imagination that recalled the coming of the Holy Spirit at this mighty public authentication of the messiahship of Jesus was playing, not with the idea of the dove as a harmless bird, but with the idea of the Spirit of God brooding over the waters of chaos (Gen. 1:2). What a modern Western mind would probably have said is, "It was almost as though there were a physical presence brooding there." The Oriental mind is bolder and more concrete. This was something terrifying, comparable with the awesome moment of creation itself. To express it in the astonishing words, "Softer than gale at morning prime," is at once to fall into exegetical error. And it is this error which has induced all the sentimentality about the Holy Spirit that prevails today. This is further encouraged by the use of a favorite hymn from the same period which goes to a singularly depressing tune:

> He came sweet influence to impart,
> A gracious, willing guest.
>
> . . . .
>
> And his that gentle voice we hear,
> Soft as the breath of even (H. 368).

Well, we may ask, if temptations are what Charles Wesley said they were, what use is a voice "soft as the breath of even" going to be? The dove is quite properly portrayed in Charles Wesley:

> Expand Thy wings, celestial dove,
> Brood o'er our nature's night;
> On our disordered spirits move,
> And let there now be light (CP. 226).

That gets it exactly, with explicit reference to Gen. 1:2. The only trouble remaining is that "dove" simply does not convey "the breaking forth of creation" to a modern mind. This is a case where the communication has simply broken down, and where within a generation from now it may be that the image will have to be altogether scrapped. This is a pity, because several fine hymns will have to go, or be altered, and that great verse of Wesley's, being direct exegesis, will have to disappear altogether.

Another image which seems to be a little shaky is that of "breath," as in the well-known "Breathe on me, Breath of God" (H. 375). A little reflection will cause the august scene in the upper room, recorded in John 20:22, to come to mind. "Jesus breathed on them, and said, 'Receive ye the Holy Ghost.'" The scene there recorded is too intimate to bear, or need, analysis in physical terms. But the actual words of its recording are the only reason why that excellent hymn writer, Edwin Hatch, cast his hymn in the form he did. And in doing so, beginning each verse with "Breathe on me," he runs to death an image of intimacy which just will not stand that treatment. Instead of leaving us with the idea of a Spirit of power and creativeness, he leaves us with the picture of an inhibited and diffident whispering. The rest of the hymn is so strong that its opening line, repeated in every verse, becomes increasingly incongruous. As an anthropomorphic image the true poetry of the Old Testament is better than the evangelist's simple language for creating an image of the power of God: "Then the channels of waters were seen, and the foundations of the world were discovered at thy rebuke, O Lord, at the blast of the breath of thy nostrils" (Ps. 18:15).

The hymn writers are on surer ground when their thought is theological, when they tell us of the Holy Spirit (see Appendix B, p. 176), the Advocate. "Comforter" in the King James Version is too soft altogether: "Advocate" is the word.

> There is a way for man to rise
>   To that sublime abode:
> An offering and a sacrifice,
> A Holy Spirit's energies,
>   An Advocate with God.
>
> . . . .
>
> These, these prepare us for the sight
>   Of holiness above (H. 478).

But we must beware of all hymns which reduce the Holy Spirit to a polite, domestic creature that can be led around by any pious hypocrite and called on for guidance by any arrogant schismatic. It is a fact of church history that few heresies, puritanical schisms, or religious deviations have not claimed in vociferous terms the special advocacy of the Holy Spirit. It is not surprising that in our own time the pattern of these old heresies repeats itself so emphatically. The hymns often tell us just this about the Holy Spirit.

2. The True
Poetry of Scripture

In contrast to the somewhat mournful material we have been considering, let us now examine some of the best examples among well-known hymns of the use of imagery that comes from the Bible. These examples we will choose with care, because they are meant to be examples of imagery which, even though it be not always immediately comprehensible, can easily be explained by reference to the Bible, and at no stage causes offense or difficulty to the singer. We shall keep the other poetic devices for a later stage, here confining ourselves as much as we can to the hymns which take their illumination from the Bible.

"Wachet Auf"

First, consider one of the most ancient of reformation hymns, which was originally written in German—the immortal "Wachet auf." I shall here give it in a composite translation; the literary outrage of this will be here compensated by the fact that in this form the hymn in English reflects as much as possible of the imagery of the original German. The first two verses are given in the translation of Francis C. Burkitt (EH. 12), and the last in that of Frances E. Cox (HAM. 1958, 55). The translation of Catherine Winkworth which is much used in the United States (H. 3), though good writing, omits a great deal of the color of the original.

> Wake, O wake! with tidings thrilling
> The watchmen all the air are filling,
> Arise, Jerusalem, arise!

Midnight strikes! no more delaying,
"The hour has come!" we hear them saying.
　　Where are ye all, ye virgins wise?
　　　　The Bridegroom comes in sight,
　　　　Raise high your torches bright!
　　　　　　Alleluya!
　　　　The wedding song
　　　　Swells loud and strong:
　　Go forth and join the festal throng.

Sion hears the watchmen shouting,
Her heart leaps up with joy undoubting,
　　She stands and waits with eager eyes;
See her Friend from heaven descending,
Adorned with truth and grace unending!
　　Her light burns clear, her star doth rise.
　　　　Now come, thou precious Crown,
　　　　Lord Jesu, God's own Son!
　　　　　　Hosanna!
　　　　Let us prepare
　　　　To follow there,
　　Where in thy Supper we may share.

Praise to him who goes before us!
Let men and angels join in chorus,
　　Let harp and cymbal add their sound.
Twelve the gates, a pearl each portal—
We haste to join the choir immortal
　　Within the Holy City's bound.
　　　　Ear ne'er heard aught like this,
　　　　Nor heart conceived such bliss,
　　　　　　Alleluia!
　　　　We raise the song,
　　　　We swell the throng,
　　To praise thee ages all along.

There, of course, is one of the perfect hymns of all time. It conveys, first, a single overall impression of pageantry, energy, light, color, and expectancy. This is entirely faithful to the biblical teaching about the relation between the temporal world and the eternal world. The total impression is gained by a succession of images, every one of which is biblical.

First, the prophetic note, "Awake, awake, . . . O Zion" (Isa. 52:1). Then at once the image of the five wise virgins (Matt. 25:1-13) is superimposed, and the joy of the wedding, with the bridegroom at the center, is worked out. The bridesmaids are still outside; the joy is still waited for, but it is imminent. Then in the second stanza the imagery of the book of Revelation is added: in Rev. 21:2, the New Jerusalem descends "as a bride adorned for her husband." But the profounder thought is of the love of Christ for his church, foreshadowed in the bridal imagery of Isaiah 52, worked out in the same terms in Ephesians 5. The bridal imagery fades from bridesmaid to bride, and the idea of God tabernacling with men from Revelation 21 completes the thought of the church waiting for her bridegroom. The bridal feast is the Eucharist, the "marriage supper of the Lamb" (Rev. 19:7-9). In the third stanza more color is added—color and sound: the twelve gates, each like a pearl (Rev. 21:21), the immortal choir (Rev. 5:14), and a comment from I Cor. 2:9, "Eye hath not seen, nor ear heard." In the German original the last two lines break into merry Latin:

> Dess sind wir froh, i-o, i-o!
> Ewig in dulci iubilo.

English cannot rise to that; but notice how the poet and his translators have worked out the implications of expectancy and joy in terms of three quite clear biblical images. This is great writing, not least because of its restraint. The bold lines of the drawing make a great picture. In Charles Wesley we often find a richer biblical allusion; indeed, to sort out the allusions in some of his hymns is like separating the tiny pieces of a large mosaic. But Philip Nicolai in 1596, when he wrote this heraldic hymn and the tune that goes with it, gave the church a perfect example of hymn writing which sounds as fresh now as it did when he wrote it. This is primarily because his images, colorful though they are, are strictly governed by reason, and are thus built into a truly poetic structure.

"The Church's one foundation"

Now consider "The Church's one foundation," a hymn written more than two and a half centuries after "Wachet auf." Its first three stanzas are a model of sound yet lyrical writing.

The Church's one foundation
  Is Jesus Christ her Lord;
She is his new creation
  By water and the word.
From heav'n he came and sought her
  To be his holy bride;
With his own blood he bought her,
  And for her life he died.

Elect from ev'ry nation,
  Yet one o'er all the earth,
Her charter of salvation,
  One Lord, one faith, one birth;
One holy Name she blesses,
  Partakes one holy food,
And to one hope she presses,
  With ev'ry grace endued.

Though with a scornful wonder
  Men see her sore oppresst,
By schisms rent asunder,
  By heresies distresst;
Yet saints their watch are keeping,
  Their cry goes up, "How long?"
And soon the night of weeping
  Shall be the morn of song (H. 396).

Once again, what is to be noticed is an economy rather than a richness of imagery. The opening verse is a plain theological statement
in verse, using phrases that bring to mind several key passages in
Scripture: "Other foundation can no man lay" (I Cor. 3:11); "That
he might sanctify and cleanse it with the washing of water by the
word" (Eph. 5:26); "Christ also loved the church and gave himself
for it" (Eph. 5:25). Then in the second stanza comes the picture of
the worldwide church in its essential unity, with reminiscences of
Eph. 4:4-7. In the third stanza we have a contrasted image of the
church divided, brought to a point by that most telling quotation
from Rev. 6:10, "And they cried with a loud voice, saying, How
long, O Lord?" which itself echoes Ps. 13:1 and other utterances in
the Psalms. The rest of the hymn falls away, perhaps from this high

distinction, and it ends on a commonplace note. But in those three stanzas is real writing. Skillfully combined and contrasted pictures drive home the essential message of the hymn. It is interesting, though it is quite unnecessary, to know that it was written by a young Anglican priest who was shocked by the Colenso-Gray controversy which was dividing his church at the time. Even if one does not know that, the hymn is moving and cogent.

"There is a land of pure delight"

Now let us see how Isaac Watts, that prince of hymn writers, does it. "There is a land of pure delight" is his nearest approach to romantic poetry in hymnody, perhaps the richest of all his hymns in many-faceted imagery.

> There is a land of pure delight,
>   Where saints immortal reign;
> Eternal day excludes the night,
>   And pleasures banish pain.
>
> There everlasting spring abides,
>   And never-fading flowers;
> Death, like a narrow sea, divides
>   This heav'nly land from ours.
>
> Bright fields beyond that swelling flood
>   Stand dressed in living green;
> So to the Jews fair Canaan stood,
>   While Jordan rolled between.
>
> But timorous mortals start and shrink
>   To cross the narrow sea;
> And linger, trembling on the brink,
>   And fear to launch away.
>
> O could we make our doubts remove,
>   Those gloomy doubts that rise,
> And see the Canaan that we love,
>   With faith's illumined eyes:
>
> Could we but climb where Moses stood,
>   And view the landscape o'er,

Not Jordan's stream, nor death's cold flood,
Should fright us from the shore (H. 586).

This is a most unusual piece of writing for Watts, who was usually so sternly Calvinist in his habits, for from beginning to end it does not mention the name of God or of Christ. In a lesser writer the result would very probably be but half Christian. But more than that, Watts deliberately superimposes a biblical image on another image which lies rather in the field of pre-Christian religion, and which (very surprisingly) is most sharply illuminated by modern psychology.

He is writing about death, and encouraging the Christian not to fear it. It is believed that he was moved to write about it in these terms by the sight of the Isle of Wight across the narrow strait that divides it from the mainland (although some say that he was standing on the left bank of the Humber, near Hessle, East Yorkshire, and looking over towards the fields of Lincolnshire). However that may be, he takes the image of *water* to represent death.

Now this is an image straight from the exodus. The Red Sea (Exodus 14) and the Jordan (Joshua 4) equally represented, in the mythology of Hebrew thinking, the supreme crisis of death. Standing as they do at the beginning and at the end of the journey to the "Promised Land," these two stretches of water induced an ambivalent fear in the Israelites when they came to them. In each case these people, who were escaping from a bitter bondage, saw a barrier between them and their goal so formidable that they were inclined to say, "Promised land or no, we cannot reach it at *this* cost." It is not difficult to see how the crisis of death, despite the promise of heaven that lies beyond it for the Christian believer, follows the same pattern. Watts introduces, with Miltonic aptness, proper names like Moses and Canaan to bring the exodus story vividly before us.

But of course this is not only biblical, for there is also the myth in classical Greek and Roman religions of the river Styx across which souls are ferried to Hades by the boatman Charon. And nowadays we have from the psychologists the assurance that dreams about water in large expanses (river, sea, and such pictures) have a deep symbolism of crisis.

This is unusually interesting, because it shows how a biblical

41

mythology, which is uppermost in such a hymn as this, can chime with a truth which in biblical times, and in the time when the poem was written, still lay hidden. But Watts keeps it biblical.

This may be instructively compared with lines by a very different kind of poet on the same theme:

> And so beside the silent sea
> I wait the muffled oar;
> No harm from him can come to me
> On ocean or on shore.
>
> I know not where his islands lift
> Their fronded palms in air;
> I only know I cannot drift
> Beyond his love and care (H. 441, sts. 4-5).

Whittier in that poem (which, to be fair, was not designed for singing as a hymn) commits himself to Charon and Styx, and to the "Islands of the blessed," but not to the book of Exodus. The water image is there in the "sea" and the "Islands," but nothing in the poem makes it Christian. Watts is more penetrating because he makes such fruitful use of the Bible; and, what is more, the connection between the Exodus and the Christian Easter is so strong in biblical thinking that the singer can easily supply for himself the key proposition, which is that because Christ is risen, we need not fear death.

Watts is not usually so allusive as this. Normally he uses propositions rather than images, and writes very close to the Bible in extended passages. But here he foreshadows the art which later hymn writers were to use with such fertility—and with such capacity for error.

"Come, O thou Traveller"

Charles Wesley, of course, is the world's most versatile master of poetic device in hymnody. There are so many ways in which his gifts could be illustrated at their best (and many examples could be given of his capacity for the obscure or the tendentious); we will be content with two contrasted hymns. Here are the four stanzas of his twelve-stanza poem, "Wrestling Jacob," which are commonly found in hymnbooks. Different books give different selections; none but the English *Methodist Hymn-Book* gives the whole. Not only could it not be sung nowadays in its entirety, but it is highly doubtful whether Charles Wesley designed it for singing: for many of what are known as his hymns are really poems, meditations, or teaching lyrics.[1] It will therefore be enough to give as much of the hymn as singers usually see in their books.

> Come, O thou Traveller unknown,
>   Whom still I hold, but cannot see,
> My company before is gone,
>   And I am left alone with thee;
> With thee all night I mean to stay,
> And wrestle till the break of day.
>
> I need not tell thee who I am,
>   My misery or sin declare;
> Thyself hast called me by my name;
>   Look on thy hands, and read it there!
> But who, I ask thee, who art thou?
> Tell me thy name, and tell me now.
>
> [A stanza omitted here]
>
> Yield to me now, for I am weak,
>   But confident in self-despair;
> Speak to my heart, in blessings speak,
>   Be conquered by my instant prayer!
> Speak, or thou never hence shalt move,
> And tell me if thy name is Love.
>
> 'Tis Love! 'Tis Love! Thou diedst for me!
>   I hear thy whisper in my heart!
> The morning breaks, the shadows flee;
>   Pure universal Love thou art!
> To me, to all, thy mercies move;
> Thy nature and thy name is Love (EH. 378).

[1] On this, see the very interesting introduction to Frank Baker's *Representative Verse of Charles Wesley* (Nashville: Abingdon Press, 1962).

There is much dispute among editors on the question of whether this ought to be sung as a hymn, and much dispute among musicians as to what is the right tune for it. I am here defending its use as a hymn and its inclusion in hymnals, because I believe that here you have a hymn whose deep mysterious language will unerringly lead the singer toward a depth of faith which no other hymn can quite achieve for him.

I should like for a moment to be autobiographical here, because it will help me to make my point. I first heard this hymn when I was thirteen, at school, sung to a peculiarly arresting homemade tune (since printed, by the way, as No. 496 in *Congregational Praise*, where it is called "Cotswold"). I can seldom remember being so profoundly moved by a hymn at the first time of singing. Partly it was the tune, but partly also—my memory has never lost hold of this —it was the word "traveller" in the opening line. I am now pretty sure that Wesley used the word "traveller" as a neutral apposition for this mysterious angel of Peniel. But to a youngster of the earlier twentieth century "traveller" at once spelled romance. This is important, I think, because it compensates for the unhappy depression of the meaning of "bosom," which we had to notice earlier. Images can attach themselves to words after the words have been put down by their authors. If they do and they are good, it is entirely to the benefit of the hymn. Thus attracted, as I remember, I was never put off by the obscurity of the rest of the hymn. I was, on the contrary, intrigued. I wondered who was addressing whom, and what on earth about. It was a great day when—years later, of course—I found that it was all there in Genesis 32. But in the meantime there was something in the wrestling and struggling that came through the hymn that suggested all the time that it is a representation of a young man's discovery of Christ. Jacob in Genesis 32 was middle-aged and a substantial citizen, but he discovered that night something which left him weaker, yet immeasurably stronger. Wesley thinks that he saw straight forward to the redemption of the Crucified (see st. 2, l. 4). This conceit he uses to enable the singer to place himself where Jacob was and avail himself of the same redemption.

I do not feel that obscurity in itself is a reason why images should be discarded or why hymns should not be sung. Provided the real depth of the thought can be seen to be reasonable and based on right teaching, the right thing to do is to find the right tune and let the people sing until, after years of singing, the real joy of discovery breaks through.

"Love divine"

This is not the only time Wesley uses this image of "I will not let thee go unless thou bless me!"; it comes again in an equally beautiful though much simpler hymn (see Appendix B, pp. 176-177), "Shepherd divine, our wants relieve" (CP. 494). But let us now turn to an example of a more familiar style in Wesley—the biblical mosaic. This is another way in which he was capable of providing infinitely more than a singer could pick up at first hearing, and thus making room for the increase of discovery and understanding through repeated singings. We will extract as many biblical references as we can from one of his most celebrated hymns.

> Love divine, all loves excelling,
>   Joy of heaven, to earth come down,
> Fix in us thy humble dwelling (Rev. 21:3),
>   All thy faithful mercies crown.
> Jesus, thou art all compassion,
>   Pure, unbounded love thou art;
> Visit us with thy salvation (Ps. 106:4),
>   Enter ev'ry trembling heart (Deut. 28:65).
>
> Come, almighty to deliver
>   Let us all thy life receive (John 3:16),
> Suddenly return, and never (Mal. 3:1),
>   Nevermore thy temples leave.
> Thee we would be always blessing (Ps. 84:4),
>   Serve thee as thy hosts above,
> Pray, and praise thee without ceasing,
>   Glory in thy perfect love.
>
> Finish then thy new creation; (Phil. 1:6; II Cor. 5:17)
>   Pure and spotless let us be: (James 1:27)
> Let us see thy great salvation
>   Perfectly restored in thee. (Ps. 51:12; Acts 1:6)
> Changed from glory into glory, (II Cor. 3:18)
>   Till in heav'n we take our place,

> Till we cast our crowns before thee, (Rev. 4:10)
> Lost in wonder, love, and praise (H. 478).

Here we have, many times in each stanza, reminiscences of scriptural expressions which bring to mind the many-sided doctrine of Christian perfection, Wesley's subject in this hymn. To master all these texts would take a long time; to pick up every allusion, even to a devout eighteenth-century Christian, would be virtually impossible. But for all that, the impression that the hymn always leaves is one of brilliance and color. It is worth observing one reason why it makes so deep an impact even on those who are far from following its author's thought at all closely. Wesley lived not only in the eternal world but in this one. He was particularly fond of the music of Henry Purcell and the ceremonious poetry of his time. This he shows in his first and last lines: for "Love divine, all loves excelling" is a direct adaptation of a verse by John Dryden beginning, "Fairest isle, all isles excelling," and Purcell's tune to that song was what Wesley hoped would become the tune to his hymn. (It was indeed sung occasionally in the author's lifetime, and was set to the words in the first musical setting they received.) This then is an image taken from a purely secular source. And the last line is similarly lifted directly from Addison, who in 1712 had used it as the closing line of his hymn, "When all thy mercies, O my God" (H. 297). The mosaic of biblical images is actually framed in phrases taken from nonbiblical sources, and human art comes to the help of sacred exposition. This is inspired work indeed. It is very far from the pedestrian poetry which so often has to pass for praise in our hymnbooks.

It must be noted before we leave Wesley that the former of these hymns, "Come, O thou Traveller," contained one image which has passed far out of sacred, and even polite, modern usage. Unless one wants to court ridicule, one cannot print the penultimate line of the fourth verse (in our abridgment) as Wesley wrote it; for where we have "mercies," he has "bowels," a sound biblical word but an impossible notion to present-day singers. What is surprising, of course, is that this kind of thing does not happen more often than it does: and, if we may introduce a quite irrelevant aside, it is even more astonishing to find how much less often this happens in the language of the English *Book of Common Prayer* (chiefly 1549) than it happens even in the King James Version (1611). On the other hand, the word "life" in "Love divine," (vs. 2, line 2) may be unfamiliar to singers in general, but this was Wesley's word, changed early but unnecessarily to "grace." The filling of the soul with the "life of God" was a common notion in Wesley, and it is an idea central to the gospel.

Both these hymns, however, give us occasion to emphasize the point that so long as the ideas are connected to the images by right exegesis, and the whole composition is held together by reason, there is no limit to the depth to which it can go, and no author's work ought to be discarded just because it appears "difficult." It is all the better for providing more and more light and truth each time it is sung, and none the worse if it demands a decent understanding of the Bible for its interpretation.

3. The
Images of Mythology

Myth and Demythologization

Perhaps it is a pity that the most important controversy of recent years in the biblical field carries the terrifying label of "demythologization." That cannot be helped. I myself believe it to be so important—and believe it also to be essentially so easy for any intelligent layman to understand—that I wish to ask for my reader's attention to it here. The author of the controversial statement on demythologization is Rudolf Bultmann, and in order to state the terms of the matter as economically and simply as they can be stated, I shall quote from a very useful recent paper on the subject. This will put the reader abreast of the subject, should he be of those who think that a controversy so formidably labeled is something merely academic. The following paragraphs are quoted from Ian Henderson's *Myth in the New Testament* commenting on Bultmann's essay, *Neues Testament und Mythologie.*

The essay begins with the assertion that the picture of the world that we find in the New Testament is a mythological one. The universe, as the New Testament writers see it, is a three-decker affair, conceived quite literally in spatial terms. On the top flat [In Scottish speech "top flat" means "top floor" or "top story."] is heaven, in the middle is the earth, and down below in Sheol, Hades, the Underworld. But the middle flat is, so to speak, not self-contained, for both God from on high and the demons from below have access to it. The demons can possess men, as we find in the thought of the Synoptic Gospels. God too can speak to men and lend them the supernatural power of His spirit. Man, thus exposed in the inmost sanctuary of his being to the invasion of other spirits, can hardly be said to be his own master. In the realm of nature, this intervention from above and below means that the earth is anything but the scene of order and natural law envisaged by nineteenth century physics. The course of the history of this world is further thought of as dominated by beings whose habitat lies outside its bounds. The present era is thought of as subject to Satan and the "powers" of sin and death. It is hastening towards an end amid all the attendant woes which such a cosmic catastrophe will bring to humans.

When the New Testament goes on to describe the saving action of God in Jesus Christ, which is its main theme, as it is that of the Christian message today, it describes this action in terms of the contemporary mythological conception of the world. This mythology has two sources, Gnosticism and Jewish Apocalyptic, and the coming and work of Jesus Christ are described by means of concepts which come from one or other of them. He is described as a pre-existent Divine being whose coming marks the end of the present era. By His death He obtains atonement for the sins of men; His resurrection means that death is despoiled of its power. The demonic world powers are thus robbed of this dominion and the beginning of the end of the present era is ushered in. Meanwhile Christ is conceived of as ascending to a heaven quite literally thought of as located above the earth. He will, according to the New Testament writers, shortly return from there on the clouds to complete His work and finally to destroy sin and death and suffering. Until then, those who belong to the Church are joined to Him through the sacraments of Baptism and Holy Communion. Further, in the Spirit which works in them they have the pledge which attests that they are children of God and assures them of their resurrection.

All this, says Bultmann flatly, is mythology. It was natural for the gospel to be stated in these terms, for that was the outlook of the age. But it is not the outlook of this age.[1]

What I here want to draw attention to is the fact that whether this expositor of Bultmann's view of the gospel can or cannot get this summary of it from the Bible, without doubt he could have got it

[1] (London: S.C.M. Press, 1952), pp. 10-11. Used by permission.

from any hymnbook. The great question is being asked, whether or not we must reframe our whole statement of faith so as to tie it less closely to the thought forms of a prescientific age and more closely to those of the age in which we and our hearers live. About this at the biblical and homiletical level there is much debate which here we must leave aside. But anyone who has listened to preachers of our age knows the difference between the preacher who uses the language, the vocabulary, and the thought forms of the New Testament writers, and the preacher who, having given them up as useless, substitutes not only the language but also the doctrines of present-day Western civilization for the gospel. The liberal movement asked the great questions about the gospel, and gave the answer that the whole gospel must be restated. But in its restatement it guarded insufficiently against the danger of stating not the gospel but something else—normal, humanistic optimism. The consequence is the appearance of sermon topics on public notices which, if I may speak naïvely and candidly as a grateful guest in the United States but not as a citizen of that country, I have often found hair-raising in their brash assumption that the old gospel themes have had their day. Against this there is a fundamentalist reaction which says in effect, "If the people have faith, understanding sufficient for their needs will come," and which often closes its mind to the questions which any six-year-old wants to ask about the ascension.

Bultmann, even if his methods are by now somewhat dated and his scientific assumptions easily dismissed by modern scientists, sought a middle way between the liberal rejection and the fundamentalist credulity. Not much thought is needed to bring anyone to the conclusion that the statement of the gospel in contemporary terms without distortion of is central truths is the church's whole preaching task today. The church does it very badly: but even if it did it very well, do the hymnals help the people to gain a really lively sense of the vitality of the gospel?

It will be enough if here we take a few of the more evident points in this argument, and see how far our hymns help or impede the faith of our congregations at those points. We may attend to the ascension, the atonement, the resurrection, and the apparently anti-scientific attitude associated with "demonic" theology.

Ascension

The ascension, which is where Bultmann starts, makes a good beginning because it seems, on the face of it, to be a doctrine wholly dependent on a "three-decker universe" pattern of natural philosophy. It is a doctrine which has caused so much doubt and confusion in our time that many of those whose worship is not conditioned by a rigid adherence to the church's year have quietly discarded it. In 1951, when *Congregational Praise* was being edited, the editorial committee decided against having a section headed "The Ascension," and those hymns especially associated with that season are distinguished in that book only by being placed in a separate chronological sequence from the Easter hymns; and this, if I may allow a secret to emerge where it will do no harm, was a wholly unofficial arrangement made by the subeditor who was responsible for the final order of the hymns. Many other hymnals ignore the ascension, even though they include hymns appropriate to the season.

Now there are two things we can do if we want to explain the ascension and preach from it. We can take the scriptural account absolutely literally and say that it is important to note that the Lord was levitated from the earth, and thus passed into heaven, which is above the earth. In that case we must sever any connection between religious thought and scientific and natural thought. Or we can demythologize the event. This means stripping our account of it of all secondary things which belong, in the scriptural account, to the thought of the time, but which do not really provide essential support for the doctrine.

What happens if we do this? We begin from first principles. What is it that the author of Acts is trying to describe in his first chapter? He supposes, and we also assume, that there are three possible conditions of being: that in which the Lord's will is always done; that in which it is never done; and that in which there is a strife between obedience and disobedience—a disputed ground between the two extremes. This to the ancient mind is sufficiently imaged in the three-decker universe. But even when we have discarded the idea of a three-decker physical universe, it is an elementary truth that once you have supposed that God's will exists, and that it is not always done, omnipotent though God is, you have at once a three-decker moral universe.

51

It is further supposed in Christian doctrine that Jesus, whose proper place is in that part of the moral universe where God's will is always done, came to that part where God's rule is disputed. This is, in the old picture, to say that "he came down from heaven." But his proper place is there, not here. By what means can he be supposed to have returned thither? Only by finally leaving this physical world, and not (as we shall have to say under "Resurrection" by death. The old mythology says he went "up," because the perfect world is above this one. This may or may not be historically true. What is true is that he went *away*. After all, in the universe as we know it today, what can "up" mean but "away"? We can add furthermore that the effect of his coming to the disputed ground decisively affected the place, or condition of things, in which God's will is never done; and this completely new assessment of the power that is over against the will of God is imaged in one interpretation of "He descended into hell." (Not in both: for according to another interpretation, the descent into hell was the extending to all who had died without the sight of Christ the efficacy of his redemption.)

This is an experiment in demythologization: and it is one way—surely not the only way—of interpreting the ascension to a modern mind. Believing as I do that it is a correct way, that we have removed nothing essential from the ascension by shifting the emphasis from "up" to "away," and by being agnostic about the actual direction and means of our Lord's translation from one to another of two spheres whose existence we are certain of, I would now ask, how much do our hymns help us here?

The traditional Ascension Day hymn is by Charles Wesley, "Hail the day that sees him rise." (Wesley also wrote, and in the same meter, hymns equally indivorcible from Easter and Christmas.) Originally it was a hymn in ten four-line stanzas, the alleuias being optional. In the United States it is commonly reduced to three or four, and in these many words are altered. This is the four-stanza version in the 1940 Episcopal *Hymnal* (see Appendix B, pp. 177-78) :

> Hail the day that sees him rise,
> Glorious to his native skies;
> Christ, awhile to mortals giv'n,
> Enters now the highest heav'n!

> There the glorious triumph waits;
> Lift your heads, eternal gates!
> Wide unfold the radiant scene;
> Take the King of glory in!
>
> See! he lifts his hands above;
> See! he shows the prints of love:
> Hark! his gracious lips bestow,
> Blessings on his Church below.
>
> Lord beyond our mortal sight,
> Raise our hearts to reach thy height,
> There thy face unclouded see,
> Find our heav'n of heav'ns in thee (H. 104).

This is a miserable abridgment of a spectacular original. Who on earth could have imagined that a singer could be deceived into thinking that Wesley would write a line like "Wide unfold the radiant scene"? The original—which does seem quite inoffensive—is "Conqueror over death and sin." In the last stanza here given, English syntax is violated. For what is the construction of the word "see"? Wesley originally wrote:

> Grant, though parted from our sight,
> High above yon azure height,
> Grant our hearts may thither rise,
> Following thee beyond the skies.

One can see where that verse seemed patient of alteration: but not at the expense of English. However, even these editors have not been able to extinguish Wesley's fire entirely, and what we do have still is a perfectly clear assumption of rising to the sky. In the second stanza there is an allusion to the twenty-fourth Psalm, which in the church's liturgy is associated with this season, and which itself provides a mysterious but powerful image. In the third stanza there is a reference to Christ's blessing of the disciples, in Luke's first account of the event (at the end of his Gospel); and in the fourth stanza there is a verbal reminiscence of the collect for Ascension Day. In the original there are other biblical references, including one to the passage in II Kings 2 where Elisha parts from Elijah, and the bystanders said, "Knowest thou that the Lord will take away thy master from thy head to day?" vs. 5, and linking it up with the angel's words in Acts: "Why stand ye gazing up into heaven?" Now biblical typology, such as the usage here (and in other hymns of the ascension) of the twenty-fourth Psalm, is an excellent way of building up faith, and in this case liturgy hallows it. But the hard core of primitive natural belief remains: it is the sky to which the Lord goes. The singer must be aware that sky is a symbol for eternity, unless he is to sing what he can only believe by deceiving himself. Therefore it would have been better to print the lines as Wesley originally wrote them, because they are better literature than what editors have made of him, and because even in the adaptation the mythology of sky remains.

It is worth while to contrast Wesley's hymn with one written somewhat later, but still in an age of prescientific church belief—Thomas Kelly's "The head that once was crowned with thorns" (H. 106). In that hymn—I have elsewhere recorded the view that it is the greatest of all, and I stand by that—there is not a line of mythology. "The highest place," said Kelly. Yes, and it is not too much to ask the most obstinate of scientific fundamentalists to accept "high" for "authority." That apart, it is straight doctrine, linking the church's earthly business with Christ's eternal victory. It could be done in the 1820's—and that is something to note.

An impressive, if rather self-conscious, attempt at remythologizing the ascension is in Howard Chandler Robbins' "And have the bright immensities":

> And have the bright immensities
> Received our risen Lord,
> Where light-years frame the Pleiades
> And point Orion's sword?
> Do flaming suns his footsteps trace
> Through corridors sublime,
> The Lord of interstellar space
> And Conqueror of time?
>
> The heaven that hides him from our sight
> Knows neither near nor far:

> An altar candle sheds its light
>   As surely as a star;
> And where his loving people meet
>   To share the gift divine,
> There stands he with unhurrying feet;
>   There heavenly splendors shine (H. 354).

These unconventional lines make a deep impression: they do at least substitute words familiar to modern science for the old images of the Scriptures. Whether the hymn will prove to be of lasting value is, however, uncertain. It does really say, albeit in modern language, that the Lord has gone "to the sky"; and its second verse has a certain romantic touch that disappoints the expectations of the first. The exact sense of "There stands he with unhurrying feet" is obscure; one can picture a figure walking, but not standing, so. This is a brave attempt to remythologize the ascension, but it has not really done it. Somehow it is a shade too literal, and one might well prefer the bold image in Mrs. Alexander's paraphrase of "St. Patrick's Breastplate" (see Appendix B, pp. 178-79):

> His bursting from the spiced tomb;
>   His riding up the heavenly way (H. 268, st. 2).

"Riding" suggests again the twenty-fourth Psalm, which is an image clear of physical and scientific perplexities.

There is indeed a case for saying that George Wither, in 1623, more nearly succeeded. His ascension hymn (quoted in full below) is singularly free of dubious mythology: it refers again to the twenty-fourth Psalm, and to the collect for Ascension Day, but is not committed to anything more specific. Stanzas 1, 4, and 5 of this poem are known in Britain (CP. 151), though not, I believe, in the United States. But the whole hymn is wonderfully clear and unmythological:

> To God, with heart and cheerful voice
>   A triumph song we sing;
> And with true thankful hearts rejoice
>   In our almighty King;
> Yea to His glory we record,
>   Who were but dust and clay,

55

What honour He did us afford
  On His ascending day

The human nature, which of late
  Beneath the angels was,
Now raised from that meaner state,
  Above them hath a place.
And at man's feet all creatures bow,
  Which through the whole world be,
For at God's right hand throned now
  In glory sitteth he.

Our Lord, and Brother, who hath on
  Such flesh, as this we wear,
Before us unto Heaven is gone,
  To get us places there;
Captivity was captiv'd then,
  And he doth from above
Send ghostly presents down to men
  For tokens of his love.

Each door and everlasting gate
  To him hath lifted been;
And in a glorious wise thereat
  Our King is entered in.
Whom if to follow we regard,
  With ease we safely may,
For he hath all the means prepared,
  And made an open way.

Then follow, follow on apace,
  And let us not forego
Our Captain, till we win the place
  That He hath scaled unto:
And for His honour, let our voice
  A shout so hearty make,
The heavens may at our mirth rejoice,
  And earth and hell may shake.

There are occasional linguistic difficulties here, like "ghostly" and perhaps "dust and clay"; but the combination of creaturely merriment with biblical teaching (in addition to the references already mentioned, there are reminiscences of Psalm 8, Heb. 1:3, Ps. 68:18, and Eph. 4:8-9) makes a highly satisfying hymn. Much the same could be said of Christopher Wordsworth's excellent hymn, "See the conqueror mounts in triumph" (H. 103), which again stresses the exaltation of human nature at the ascension.

Resurrection

When we come to the resurrection, the first necessity is to be clear about the true place of the Easter hymn in the church's teaching. In those communions which take a liberal attitude to liturgy, Easter and the ascension are often confused. Although some may believe that the two events are part of a single divine act, the teaching purposes of ascension and Easter in the church's year are quite distinct. The teaching of the ascension concerns the universal reign of Christ, already sealed and later to be consummated; that of Easter concerns his specific conquest of death.

The second thing to say is that here more than anywhere else in the hymnbook a healthy faith is served by our hymns.

If we look over the Easter hymns in common use, we find that the images most commonly met with are that of *victory* and that of *renewal of life*. Easter is a creaturely season, in that its associations with springtime are much more soundly founded in history than are those of Christmas with winter; and therefore the springtime note of joy and eagerness is never far from the best Easter hymns. "Welcome, happy morning!" (H. 87) has it—and what a pity it is that such simple and innocent words are wedded to so lamentably tawdry a tune! Far better if it be sung to a strong tune in four lines, like "Evelyns" (H. 356, 2nd tune), omitting the refrain line. "The whole bright world rejoices now" (P. 194) strikes the same note. But Easter is also a season in which we recall all the patterns of victory that are set up in the Old Testament. Two texts are especially associated with this, the chapters in Exodus recording the crossing of the Red Sea and the verse in Hosea which is the origin of Paul's great cry, "O death, where is thy sting?" The exodus has its place in the Easter liturgies—Psalm 114 is the Easter psalm by tradition; and this is reflected in such hymns as "The day of resurrection!" (H. 96, P. 192), and "Come, ye faithful, raise the strain" (H. 94,

P. 185). The specific note of comfort in the face of death is heard in "Jesus lives!" (H. 88.)

It may well be said that many sincere believers entertain serious doubts about the historical facts of the resurrection, the kind of facts which we are invited to accept as true in such hymns as "O sons and daughters" (H. 99, P. 191), "Christians, to the Paschal victim" (H. 97), and certain lines of Charles Wesley's "Christ the Lord is risen today" (H. 95, P. 182). In spite of the biblical evidences, many today are inclined to doubt whether Jesus really could have left the tomb and appeared to mortals after his resurrection. These doubts are based on modern physical doctrines, and did not occur to those who lived before modern science took shape. Fearing to express such doubts, many believers are inclined to relegate them to the region where superstitions flourish.

Two things need to be said about this. The first is that as a matter of fact this is not a case of the same kind as the ascension. The ascension is an event, or a principle, which believers have largely laid aside because of its scientific difficulties, and which can be rescued by demythologization because its chief difficulty, indeed, its only important difficulty, is one of images. But at Easter there is a complex of teaching, in only one part of which a modern believer finds its difficult to believe *because he is a modern believer.* There is much besides the empty tomb and the appearances which is no more difficult for a modern believer than it was for an ancient one. Easter is not only the season when we recall (if it be right to recall) the historic events. It is much more the season when our minds are directed by the church to the *principle* of resurrection, which is something much more fundamental. Recently a book of radical criticism of the traditional teaching about the resurrection was written by a church of Scotland minister,[2] who urges us to attend primarily to the "resurrection as conviction" rather than to "the resurrection as history." His argument goes much further than many will wish to follow him. But at least he is pleading for us to recognize the profound difficulties which the naïve believer has concerning the resurrection; and he is in the excellent company of the apostle Paul himself. For in I Corinthians 15 what does Paul do but explain

[2] James McLeman, *The Birth of Christian Faith* (Edinburgh: Oliver & Boyd, 1962).

to a set of very naïve, not to say obstinate, believers at Corinth that resurrection must be thought of in at least three planes—the historic resurrection of Christ, the resurrection to which the individual believer may look forward at his own death, and that resurrection which is conversion, and which can be known in this earthly life.

We live, as we must suppose, neither in the primitive age nor in the last age. It may be true that just now, when we happen to be so full of the discoveries of modern science, we must permit a certain agnosticism about the historical facts of the resurrection. Many people will be happy to believe in them as the gospels set them down, but if there are doubts, these doubts must not be dismissed as unbelief in the central truth of the Christian faith. For the real truth of which the gospel stories may possibly be no more than the best images or symbols that human art can devise is that God is the master of death, that he can conquer, enslave, and glorify it. Toward this truth they were feeling their way in the Old Testament: the exodus and the prophets are much concerned with it. Not with personal survival and immortality—of which, despite such protests as Ps. 30:9 or such gestures of faith as Job 19:26-7, the Old Testament mind had no notion; that is a different matter. The great matter is that God is the master of death, which, if one believes, makes all the difference to one's outlook on everything in created life.

The superstition into which the naïve mind may fall at Easter time, in consequence of inadequate teaching, is that "there must be some life after death." About ten years ago a social survey was conducted in England, which was published under the title *English Life and Leisure,* by B. S. Rowntree and G. R. Lavers. In the two hundred case histories that form the book's most significant chapter it is astonishing how many people, questioned about religion, made it clear that although they had no religion, they felt there must be something in it because "there must be some life after death." People who talk so are expressing a belief that they hold because they want to hold it. The short answer to this is to say quite firmly that hymns which celebrate the felicities of eternal life will evoke much intellectual dishonesty if they do not explicitly state, or if their context in worship does not explicitly state, that there is a direct connection between that felicity and the atonement wrought by Jesus Christ.

And this is where we come to the heart of the matter. Easter hymns, when they express the fullness of joy in Christ's victory and lead us through that to rejoice in God our Maker, are entirely good. We are not required to demythologize anything, only to emphasize the universal truth of which the resurrection is itself a symbol, the truth that God conquers, enslaves, *and glorifies* death. But it is when we reach the atonement that we come to the heart of many of our troubles. It is superstition about the atonement, not superstition about resurrection, that really damages our people.

The Atonement

We have here a quite fresh set of circumstances again—different both from those which impede our belief in the ascension and from those which give us difficulties about the resurrection. Here modern science is silent. Here we have a historical fact attested by heathen authorities quite apart from the Bible. There was a crucifixion in which Jesus was judicially murdered for reasons given out as political but really religious. Nobody contests that—nobody, except certain persons, chiefly of Muhammadan views, who still believe that at the last moment another was substituted for Jesus, and that Jesus, therefore, did not die. We are spreading our net fairly wide, but we are stopping short of eccentricities like that.

But what does the crucifixion *mean* to successive generations of the church? That is the great question.

To the apostle Paul, it meant victory. Nothing else and nothing less. When he said he preached Christ's cross, he meant preaching God's power and wisdom. But whose victory, and over precisely what? The early church evaluated this in terms of the devil, the head of all the evil spirits who, gathered in their strength, sought to overthrow God's rule. To some it appeared that God paid a ransom to the devil, in the person of his Son. The objection to this theory is that it is too closely dependent on mythology. The devil is there represented as a person who will, in consideration of such payment, call off his assault on the world; or perhaps as a person whose demands, though outrageous, are technically within the bounds of justice. Now in our own time the great demythologizer of the devil is, of course, C. S. Lewis, who in his *Screwtape Letters* represents the devil as wholly corrupt, by turns cringing and bullying. The same writer has shown, following Charles Williams, that even Milton's Satan in *Paradise Lost* is not the august figure which a hasty reader might take him for. But we now want to go much further than Milton. We cannot tolerate "ransom to the devil," because the devil, so far from having any just claim or merit on which to base it, is lower than the lowest of gangsters. If he is the principle of evil, he is also, a fortiori, the principle of deceit and unreason. Ransom, to be crude, will do no good. He will only be back for more.

Ransom has, however, knit itself into sacred language, and will take a good deal of dislodging. Nonetheless, it would be wise to dislodge it if we can. It is an excellent example of a mythology which we must manage without.

Another interpretation, different but shading into that one, is of the atonement as a price paid *to God* for man's sin—a price which man could not pay for himself. This is at least tolerable in that it imputes justice to God and not to the devil. But by itself it is unsatisfactory for a number of reasons, because the connection between what I think of as my sin and the death of Christ is far from being immediately apparent unless some further teaching establishes it. If we are left with the notion that what we could not pay he has paid, we are, except something more be said, left in a condition of enslaved gratitude; for we are always told that we cannot pay him back for this. Theologically this may be admirable, but psychologically it is wholly disastrous. So is the teaching, simple and without further explanation, that "he died in our place." Following this line, preachers tell each member of their congregations that he, individually, ought to be crucified, but that Christ has been crucified in his place. Once again, what is left for human nature to do but die of shame? Is this the teaching of the Gospels?

Now many images of the atonement come from the Bible—of which those which principally cause trouble are "blood," "the Lamb," and "sacrifice." This last particularly is criticized by Bultmann as being a hangover from a bygone mythology. "Blood" means, in biblical terms, "life given." "The Lamb" is the characteristic object of sacrifice. And sacrifice itself? Well, it is not quite the crude and inhumane thing that liberals often take it for. We must beware of superimposing a humanitarian mythology on a primitive one, and ascribing to the ancients only bestial ignorance in tolerating animal sacrifice. We must make large allowance for the fact that the principle in Leviticus and other sources for the Jewish law is that man, as man, must not regard himself as having a right exclusively to what he calls his possessions: that he must always train himself to renunciation: that he must, what is more, renounce not what he can best spare, but what he can least spare, which is the best sheep in his flock. To the man Leviticus was written for, sheep were wealth; the fact that they were alive was an accident. From this source comes the notion of the "spotless Lamb."

But when all that has been allowed for, we must watch out for uses of such words as "Lamb" and "blood" and "sacrifice" in a manner that will encourage people to think sentimentally. It is possible to argue that when the idea of "priest" and that of "victim" are brought together, the idea becomes strictly Christian, as it does in certain Eucharistic hymns; but even there it must be a biblically learned congregation, one understanding the Epistle to the Hebrews, that can fasten on to the central truth thus elliptically stated.

The fact is that "Lamb" and "blood" and "sacrifice" can really be tolerated only when they are "dead metaphors." Thus, it is possible to say that "At the Lamb's high feast we sing" (H. 89) is a hymn that we can still use, because "Lamb" at once conveys "victorious Christ," and not even a picture of the lamb enters the singer's mind for an instant. On the other hand, the line "the slaughtered Lamb" in "The God of Abraham be praised" (in a stanza not now usually included in hymnals) does give pause, because the idea of slaughter is dwelt on.

> His blood can make the foulest clean
> His blood availed for me (M. 162)

may be just tolerable (although neither H. [325] nor P. [223] includes those lines in their versions of "O for a thousand tongues"), but

> There is a fountain filled with Blood
> Drawn from Emmanuel's veins (EH. 332)

is in itself beyond the reach of any imagination now, except as a repulsive image.

There is one fearful fallacy, however, that vitiates a great deal of modern popular atonement theology, which is far worse than any of those ancient and medieval arguments. It is the error of pitying the Crucified. Against this it is difficult to speak too strongly, so pervasive is it. It is, of course, the consequence of nineteenth-century romanticism; it is a new and worse mythology substituted for an old one. Where the old mythologies were unduly stern, this is sentimental. The concentration on the physical agony of the crucified, typical of nineteenth-century evangelical thinking, is unbiblical and irreligious. Psychologically nothing could be more damaging, because it induces in the believer a barren and yet insidious kind of guilt.

Consider the following passage from a book recently written on the crucifixion by an author alien to the Christian faith. He is an adherent of Islam who holds the views about the Crucified which I alluded to just now.

> To the present day, Christianity has not freed itself, and perhaps never will, from the entail of that sorrow and regret which haunted the souls of the disciples because of all that they were lacking in relationship to Christ at the time they held back from saving him. They have been destined to bear the reproach of the great sin—the sin of abandoning Christ to his foes, to his oppressors and persecutors. It seemed to them that they were only commanded to withhold themselves from rescuing their prophet because they did not deserve to be his witnesses.
>
> And thus a dread of falling into sin, an apprehensiveness about evildoing, has become a dominant feature of the Christian spirit. And so it will always remain. For Christians have no way of atoning for what happened on that day.[3]

This is precisely right, except only in the assumption that this attitude of helpless guilt is a proper and inalienable Christian attitude. If one's primary proposition about the atonement concerns the sadness and misery of the Crucified, then the next propositions concern the iniquity of those who betrayed him, arrested him, tried him, and executed him. This is, according to the gospels, a wholly wrong attitude for Christians to take. It was not even right in the "daughters

---

[3] Kamel Hussein, *City of Wrong* (London: Geoffrey Bles, Ltd., 1960), p. 121.

of Jerusalem" (Luke 23:28). Not a line in Paul vindicates it. But in many hymns of the romantic age it is insisted upon.

This must be distinguished from medieval devotions to the passion. Crude and gruesome though these sometimes were, they were invariably directed toward releasing the human soul from its guilt through the contemplation of the forgiveness that is in Christ's death. A hymn like the "Stabat Mater" (H. 76), though it dwells on the sorrows of Christ's Mother, ends in a prayer that has in it the confidence of heaven. This is different from the outright pity that we are tempted, in our day when we are (rightly, of course) so much more sensitive to human cruelty, to extend to him who reigns from the tree. Nothing can be less healthy than the guilt which it induces. It is at one point in this sensitive region that the liturgies sometimes lose their sureness of touch. On the whole it is surely unwise to include in any passiontide devotion the words from Lamentations, "Is it nothing to you, all ye that pass by?" True, they are not always so crudely and blasphemously incorporated in worship as they are in an early chorus of John Stainer's "Crucifixion," where the listener is impelled to attribute the words to Jesus. But the frequency with which, if one asks a group of Christians, "Who first said those words?" one gets the answer, "Jesus, at the crucifixion," shows how deep the error has gone in the popular mind. The speaker in the original text is, of course, Jerusalem personified—Jerusalem after it had been sacked by Babylon. To ascribe such words to the Crucified is an appalling error in typology.

The earlier devotions of the church take a quite different line. It is one of the outstanding qualities in certain medieval carols that they insist that their singers *rejoice* in the passion. The precipitous contrasts in some of these carols have proved too much for the literal-mindedness of the post-Reformation church, and in consequence they are still little known and sung. I am not sure whether some are known at all in the United States. But a glance at "All under the leaves of life," or "Awake, awake, ye drowsy souls," or "Tomorrow shall be my dancing day" (which can be found in the *Oxford Book of Carols,* Nos. 43, 44, and 71) will remind the reader how differently they looked on the passion in those days (see Appendix B, pp. 180-81).

So, of course, will "Sing, my tongue, the glorious battle" (H. 66), or "The royal banners forward go" (H. 63). Both are by the same author (see Appendix B, pp. 181-82). Both sound primarily the note of victory. Both invite our devotion to the cross in a manner paradoxical to reason (who wants to adore a common gibbet?) yet persuasive to faith. These are perhaps the greatest of all hymns on the passion, for their fiery splendor, unless "Ride on! ride on in majesty!" (H. 64, P. 175) earns the prize.

Those who have anything to do with children will perhaps have found, as I have, how many children find "There is a green hill far away" particularly distasteful. (See H. 65, P. 171.) It is largely the tune "Horsley," no doubt, whose tender beauty seems to be a strictly adult taste. But even when one has grown to love the tune—and especially then, perhaps—one increases in doubt about the terms in which this hymn puts the atonement. Particularly, when it makes us say, "He died to make us good," we can explain this only in terms of a Pauline doctrine of imputed righteousness. I must confess that I have done my best to justify this and other lines in the hymn by such references: but I must now admit that my pleading was far-fetched,[4] because the lines were written for children, and we must, I fear, admit that its author meant just what she said. It is, of course, quite wrong to say that "He died to make us good." [5]

F. W. Faber was capable of weighty sentimentality at times. The worst verses of "O come and mourn with me awhile" are now normally dropped from hymnals (H. 74. P. 164): this kind of thing is what we are now spared:

> How fast his hands and feet are nailed;
> His blessèd tongue with thirst is tied;
> His failing eyes are blind with blood:
> Jesus, our Lord, is crucified (EH. 111).

Wrath—yes. That is an emotion that, if rightly directed, we can tolerate at Passiontide. There is a magnificent hymn by Arthur Cleveland Coxe which, although it originated in America, seems not to be known there as well as it is by those who sing from *The English Hymnal:*

[4] *Hymns and the Faith* (London: John Murray, Ltd. 1955), chap. 36.
[5] For a worse example from the same author involving the word "good" see p. 77.

65

Who is this with garments gory,
    Triumphing from Bozrah's way;
This, that weareth robes of glory,
    Bright with more than victory's ray?
Who is this unwearied comer
    From his journey's sultry length,
Travelling through Idumè's summer
    In the greatness of his strength?

Wherefore red in thine apparel
    Like the conquerors of earth,
And arrayed like those who carol
    O'er the reeking vineyard's mirth?
Who art thou, the valleys seeking,
    Where our peaceful harvests wave?
"I in righteous anger speaking,
    I the mighty One to save;

"I, that of the raging heathen
    Trod the winepress all alone,
Now in victor-garlands wreathen
    Coming to redeem mine own:
I am he with sprinkled raiment,
    Glorious for my vengeance-hour,
Ransoming, with priceless payment,
    And delivering with power."

Hail! All hail: Thou Lord of Glory!
    Thee, our Father, thee we own;
Abram heard not of our story,
    Israel never our name hath known.
But, Redeemer, thou hast sought us,
    Thou hast heard thy children's wail,
Thou with thy dear Blood hast bought us:
    Hail! Thou mighty Victor, hail! (EH. 108.)

There are images to shake the dullest imagination! Dreadful though they are, they are all immediately explained by a single biblical passage—Isa. 63:1-7. Over and over again it has been shown that North Americans are the finest men of letters when it comes to writing hymns. More than half of the two dozen hymns which one could show to an agnostic man of letters without shame are by North Americans. The basic thought in this hymn is, of course, the wrath of God. Wrath is a better emotion than pity. Wrath is what Christ is recorded as showing when he saw the afflictions and distortions of human nature during his ministry. Wrath, not against man, still less against his Son, but against evil is one way of expressing the passion of God which is described in the Old Testament as "zeal" or (the same English word at bottom) "jealousy." It is not the emotion of the actual suffering human Christ, but the image of the clash between love and contempt which we see in the crucifixion. And when it is combined, as here, with "victory," we are back with the classic image of the atonement—not as tragedy, but as victory. We are back with "The royal banners."

Another fine and unusual hymn on the atonement, this time more modern, is "It is finished." In the 1940 Episcopal *Hymnal* two verses are given. I will quote here the second of those and the third which is there omitted:

> It is finished! Christ is slain,
> On the altar of creation,
> Offering for a world's salvation
>   Sacrifice of love and pain.
> Lord, thy love through pain revealing,
>   Purge our passions, scourge our vice,
> Till, upon the Tree of Healing,
>   Self is slain in sacrifice. (H. 78).

> It is finished! Christ our King
> Wins the victor's crown of glory;
> Sun and stars recite his story,
>   Floods and fields his triumph sing.
> Lord, whose praise the world is telling,
>   Lord, to whom all power is given,
> By thy death, hell's armies quelling,
>   Bring thy Saints to reign in heaven (EH. 118).

This is as good a modern interpretation of "sacrifice" as you will find in present-day hymn singing. The author is Gabriel Gillett (1873-1948) who was at one time secretary of the Society for the Propagation of the Gospel.

This kind of virile speech is not a denial but an acceptance of the fruit of the cross. It is natural, of course, that hymn writers should explore the intimacies as well as the grandeurs of the Christian doctrine of our redemption: but when they do, except they take care, they lead us astray. Isaac Watts could do it. He did it superbly in the greatest of all hymns on the atonement written since the reformation, and again in the second greatest. It may appear contentious to place the two hymns I am about to quote in this order, but I shall give reasons for doing so. I believe the greatest of all is one that is hardly known outside one or two branches of English Dissent. I have quoted it before: it is this:

> Nature with open volume stands,
>   To spread her Maker's praise abroad;
> And every labour of His hands
>   Shows something worthy of a God.
>
> But in the grace that rescued man,
>   His brightest form of glory shines;
> Here, on the cross, 'tis fairest drawn,
>   In precious blood, and crimson lines.
>
> Here His whole Name appears complete:
>   Nor wit can guess, nor reason prove,
> Which of the letters best is writ,
>   The power, the wisdom, or the love.
>
> Here I behold his inmost heart,
>   Where grace and vengeance strangely join,
> Piercing his Son with sharpest smart,
>   To make the purchas'd pleasures mine.
>
> O the sweet wonders of that cross,
>   Where God the Saviour loved, and died!
> Her noblest life my spirit draws
>   From His dear wounds, and bleeding side.
>
> I would for ever speak His Name
>   In sounds to mortal ears unknown,

68

> With angels join to praise the Lamb.
> And worship at His Father's throne (cf. CP. 129).[6]

The reader will at once wish to compare that with the more famous "When I survey the wondrous cross" (H. 337, P. 177). He will probably be unwilling to say that "When I survey" is not better. In the end the absolute judgment of priority does not matter. But attend to this other hymn first. It is unknown, whereas "When I survey" is known all over the world. Why? They are in the same meter. They could be sung to the same tune. ("When I survey," I make bold to say, has never found a truly adequate tune. That which is sung in Britain is tolerable—no more: that which is commonly sung in the United States is desperately trivial.) Part of the reason for the strange difference in popular acceptance is undoubtedly that "When I survey" projects at once the image of the Crucified to the singer's mind, whereas "Nature with open volume" keeps it until the fifth stanza.

But observe what Isaac Watts is doing in "Nature with open volume." He is projecting, in lyric form, a whole doctrine of nature and grace: he is placing the cross at the center not only of human life but of the cosmos. He is attacking the heart of the hidden truth about redemption through nature—and then through reason. In the third stanza he argues in an epigram—an epigram that comes straight from I Cor. 1:22, "Which is greatest—the power, the wisdom, or the love?" Then only does he bring the believer in—and he brings him in in a verse which is too intense, too condensed, to make good singing now. He is wrestling with "grace and vengeance"; and it is as if God were permitting his Son to undergo these horrors—not only permitting it but actively causing it—so that mankind might know felicity again. Notice how he writes "God the Saviour loved and died," where such modern hymnals as print the words always substitute "Christ my Saviour." Yes, "God the Saviour" is what the early fathers called the heresy of patripassianism. It is not God who dies, for God is immortal. Logically this is true: but it is no easier to believe that God lets his Son die. Watts meant to express in this impossible phrase the impossibility of giving expression to what

---

[6] *Hymns and Spiritual Songs* (Pittsburgh: R. Patterson & Lambdin, 1819), book III, p. 224.

really happens here. Only then, only after that immensity of mental wrestling, come praise and peace.

Now "When I survey" has no such danger point. It is a more perfect lyric. It attempts far less, and what it attempts it achieves to perfection. In this hymn too there is a verse which nowadays few people sing. It stands fourth in the original:

> His dying crimson like a robe,
>   Spreads o'er his body on the Tree;
> Then am I dead to all the globe,
>   And all the globe is dead to me (EH. 107).

The omission of this verse offends any to whom Gal. 6:14 is a living text, for it is nothing but a paraphrase of it. Yet one can understand how an unbiblical generation finds its second couplet incomprehensible. It is omitted for reasons less respectable than those which dictate the omission of the fourth stanza of "Nature with open volume." But take the whole hymn, with that verse restored, and removing foolish modesties like "offering" in the last verse for Watts's bolder "present": what you have is still a hymn whose perfection is purchased at the price of a colossal cosmic suggestiveness that the other hymn attempts. "When I survey" is a hymn of personal self-offering. It closes the question whether personal self-offering is the highest point of religion. The other hymn, complementarily, says that praise and wonder are the climax. These are two different statements; perhaps they are not mutually exclusive. It is, however, a mistake to exclude hymns that take one line and include hymns that take the other. This anticipates a point which we shall elaborate in a later chapter. Meanwhile, we must hasten to correct any impression we may have left that "When I survey" is not, in its own way, a thing of perfect beauty and of limitless suggestiveness.

4. Allegory—
True and False

The Use of Allegory

At this point it seems proper to introduce a new notion—that of *allegory*. A very familiar system of images tends by its continuity to introduce a system of *allegory*—the consistent representation by images of familiar concepts or characters. Speaking on the radio about Bunyan's immortal allegory, *The Pilgrim's Progress*, C. S. Lewis made a comment which will perhaps answer an objection that may have been forming itself in the reader's mind.

He had just been referring to the wrong way of treating an allegory, and had used one of Christ's parables to illustrate the right way of treating it. "The Foolish Virgins, within the parable, do not miss beatitude: they miss a wedding-party. The Prodigal Son, when he comes home, is not given spiritual consolations; he is given new clothes, and the best dinner his father can put up." The point is that when writing allegory, the writer (or speaker) must not at will transfer his allusions from the story to the thing which the story is meant to typify. If he is telling of wise and foolish virgins at a wedding, he must not introduce "beatitude," but must stick to the wedding, and let his hearer deduce "beatitude" from it as he deduces "wise and foolish humanity" from "wise and foolish bridesmaids." Lewis then shows how Bunyan always keeps within the story, and how insolent are those critics who think that here and there Bunyan could have improved his work by making his allusions more high-sounding or more technically Christian. And then he goes on:

This stupidity rises from the pernicious habit of reading allegory as if it were a cryptogram to be translated; as if, having grasped what an image (as we say) "means," we threw the image away and thought of the ingredient in real life which it represents . . . We ought not to be thinking, "This green valley, where the shepherd-boy is singing, represents humility." We ought to be discovering, as we read, that humility is like that green valley.[1]

Now to some extent what I have been offering in the preceding pages is a persuasive to violation of that rule. At least, it may look like that, and inasmuch as it may, I must hasten to correct it.

The best example of allegory in the Bible is, of course, the church's use of the book of Exodus. I do not say (which would certainly be wrong) that its author wrote it as allegory. But the church—and its hymn writers—have constantly, and fruitfully, used the story of the exodus as allegory. The Red Sea represents "death" or "commitment." The wilderness is "life." The journey is "our passage through life." The promised land is "heaven." The passage through the Red Sea is God's vindication of his power in the resurrection, or in your own conversion. Egypt is "hell." And so on.

But taking the standard of C. S. Lewis, we must say that to write like that is to write commentary, not to use Exodus as it should be used. He would say that the proper use of Exodus is to "discover as we read" that life is like that journey; that there is God's power, that there are real and sure promises, and that that pattern works itself out in the life of the church and the believer.

This brings us back to our immediate subject. The fact is, of course, that the naïve believer, singing hymns, treats their images and their allegory as C. S. Lewis wants them to be treated. Hymns do teach people to see life illuminated by their ideas. People quote hymns, especially in moments of stress, for their own comfort, and at such moments show how much their view of life has been colored by their singing of hymns.

But what C. S. Lewis did not have to deal with in Bunyan's case

[1] This lecture is printed in *The Listener* (November 13, 1962), p. 1007.

is the mischief that is done when the original image or allegory is a bad one, or has ceased to communicate and therefore communicates the wrong or unintended meaning. Then we are in the kind of trouble which can only be exposed by the sort of analysis we are here engaging in.

Christmas

Let us consider, by way of example, what has happened to our view of the nativity of Christ in consequence of our preference for certain kinds of hymn about that subject.

In the first place, it is worth noting that the idea of Christmas in the winter, associated with cold and especially *snow,* is a strictly European notion, associated partly with the custom inaugurated at the end of the fourth century in the Roman empire of celebrating the nativity at the time which pagan Rome gave over to the saturnalia, and partly with the undoubted fact that in Europe that time of year is midwinter (very near to the winter solstice). The association of Christmas with December 25 is venerable and entirely harmless, and only pedants would wish to change it; although there is in fact no biblical or historical warrant for its being placed there, apart from this fourth-century Roman edict, which was part of a systematic effort to replace paganism by the newly official Christian religion.

But "snow" is no part of the Christmas mythology in any Christmas carols before the vernacular carols of about the sixteenth century. One of the earliest references to it is in the carol "Es ist ein' Ros' entsprungen" (H. 17), where the events are placed *"Mittel im kalten Winter"*—"in the middle of cold winter." The older carols of the fourteenth and fifteenth centuries do not mention the season. Indeed, their preoccupation is with the incarnation, and their emphasis very often on the doctrine of the Trinity. The first verse of "In the bleak mid-winter" (H. 44, P. 128) is therefore strictly mythological. Historically, the "snow on snow" picture of Christmas was introduced into Britain from Germany in the second quarter of the nineteenth century, along with the popularization of the Christmas tree and the image of Santa Claus. The immediate question is whether this adventitious image does any harm. Of that we shall be able to judge in a moment.

73

The older and more doctrinal Christmas hymns, of course, spare us such notions. "O come, all ye faithful" (H. 12, P. 132) is as admirable an example of Roman Catholic doctrine on the incarnation as "Hark! the herald angels" (H. 27, P. 120) is of the evangelical interpretation. The other great traditional Christmas hymn, "Christians, awake" (H. 16, P. 127), is an excellent narrative paraphrase, made out of a long continuous poem in a style typical of the English eighteenth century.

But what of "It came upon the midnight clear" (EH. 19, P. 129)? Here is a fine piece of writing, set to more than one very popular tune, which does give us difficulty. There are two points at which it does this. One is where it assumes that "peace" in the song of the angels (Luke 2:15) means the cessation of earthly war (st. 3); the other is where it states in the last stanza that "the age of gold" will come "with the ever-circling years."

It would be churlish to claim that there is much harm in these somewhat sentimental Christmas lyrics. Yet something is lost when the biblical doctrine of God's reconciliation with man is obscured— a doctrine which is so clearly stated in "Hark! the herald angels." Perhaps the most positively damaging sentiment in "It came upon the midnight clear" is in its last stanza, which suggests the "return" of an "age of gold" with the "ever-circling years"—a pagan doctrine which has nothing in common with Christian eschatology.

It is rather a question of how much the sentimental Christmas hymns miss than of what harm they do. How much they miss can best be judged if we look at the richness of one of the season's profoundest and greatest hymns—"Of the Father's heart begotten." In most hymnals this is much shortened, and in some (e.g., P. 111) reduced to a fragment. The original (see Appendix B, pp. 182-84) is a very long poem associated with other subjects besides the incarnation, but a magnificent nine-verse translation by R. F. Davis appears in *The English Hymnal* (613) and *Songs of Praise* (387), and a quotation of its first six stanzas will convey the drama of the original hymn better than the examination of the truncations that most hymnals print.

> Of the Father's heart begotten,
> Ere the world from chaos rose,

He is Alpha: from that Fountain
  All that is and hath been flows;
He is Omega, of all things
  Yet to come the mystic Close,
    Evermore and evermore.

By his word was all created;
  He commanded and 'twas done;
Earth and sky and boundless ocean,
  Universe of three in one,
All that sees the moon's soft radiance,
  All that breathes beneath the sun,

He assumed this mortal body,
  Frail and feeble, doomed to die,
That the race from dust created
  Might not perish utterly,
Which the dreadful Law had sentenced
  In the depths of hell to lie,

O how blest that wondrous birthday,
  When the Maid the curse retrieved,
Brought to birth mankind's salvation,
  By the Holy Ghost conceived;
And the Babe, the world's Redeemer,
  In her loving arms received,

This is he, whom seer and sybil
  Sang in ages long gone by;
This is he of old revealèd
  In the page of prophecy;
Lo! he comes, the promised Saviour;
  Let the world his praises cry!

Sing, ye heights of heaven, his praises;
  Angels and Archangels, sing!
Wheresoe'er ye be, ye faithful,
  Let your joyous anthems ring,
Every tongue his name confessing,
  Countless voices answering,
    Evermore and evermore.

75

The point we are here making is best put thus: suppose that this hymn, in this version, were as popular as "Silent night" or "In the bleak mid-winter." Would it not have the effect of making Christians see more of what the Christmas season means? Recall C. S. Lewis' image test. The purpose of the image of the "valley of humiliation" is to make you discover that "humility is like a valley." In the same way the effect of the "snow on snow," world-brotherhood image of Christmas is to make us all think of Christmas as a season of hospitality, of child adoration, and of general bonhomie. This is quite in keeping with the secular commercialization of the season, which causes the Christmas festivities to begin some time in the middle of November and associates them chiefly with much getting and spending and eating and drinking. But the incarnation was in fact a deliverance from a *curse,* as the third stanza "Of the Father's heart begotten" says: and there was nothing sentimental or imaginary about "the curse" to the world into which the Christ child came. The blessings of the incarnation were brought not by the accident of its taking place in a stable where oxen and donkeys were sheltered, but by the obedience of the Lord's mother. The glory of the incarnation was not lessened in its being the fulfillment of so much that humanity had been groping for (st. 5). The majesty of the conception evoked by this hymn is in keeping with the majesty of the thought that it was into such a world as this that the Son of God was born. And thoughts like these, thoughts of judgment as well as mercy, of awe as well as good cheer, rebuke rather than confirm our vulgarization of the season. Christmas brings many people into touch with the church who attend it, or think of its teachings, at no other time. Partly the sentimental hymns help to achieve this. But the casual contact of many is not with the heart, or anything near the heart, of the Christmas message. It can hardly be gainsaid that nowadays the indiscriminate use of sentimental hymns and carols enhances the secularization of the season.

There ought, at any rate, to be some hymns in common use among Christians which do openly rebuke this tendency, and which require for their interpretation a committed understanding of Christmas.

There is one other well-known Christmas hymn upon which, at the risk of being thought pedantic, I feel I must offer a comment.

"Once in royal David's city" (H. 236) is in every English hymnal: it is not so universally regarded as indispensable in America. It is, for example, not in the *Pilgrim Hymnal*. In Britain it now has a special place in the national affection, being the traditional opening processional in the Service of Nine Lessons and Carols at King's College, Cambridge, which has become the pattern for similar celebrations all over the country. As sung every Christmas Eve at King's College since 1918, it has a profound, almost a hypnotic, effect. Nothing can displace it from the affections of Britishers. No hymnal editor would dare to omit it.

And it is, almost all the way, very good writing. But we have no right, nowadays, to pass over without a blushing sense of incongruity the quite unspeakable couplet:

> Christian children all must be,
> Mild, obedient, good as he.

That sentiment passed the censor in 1848 when it was first written down, but which of those three adjectives is now the more indefensible it is hard to say. The object of the couplet was to introduce a characteristically victorian moralism ("little children should be seen and not heard") into a hymn, somewhat as a disagreeable medicine may be mixed with sugar to make it palatable. "Obedient" certainly means "obedient to their mothers," and "good" equally certainly means "inconspicuous," and as for "mild," it can never have meant anything appropriate to a healthy child or baby. It is time to ask that some genius alter that couplet, or at least those three adjectives, to something more suiable for the praises of Christian parents. It had better be the whole couplet: the "must" in its first line is really the source of all the trouble. Here, anyhow, is an image that is quite intolerable, and that universally seems to go uncriticized.

Children's Hymns

It is, indeed, in the writing of children's hymns that generally modern authors and editors have shown themselves most critical of unsuitable images. And certainly in the 250 years since Isaac Watts produced the first book of hymns in English specifically for children (*Divine Songs for the Use of Children,* 1715) there have been radical changes in our attitude toward children. The chief images in the eighteenth century were associated with fear. It was, you would think to hear some of those Calvinists speaking, a sin to be young. Anyhow it was a very great danger. Being young was an experience from which you would be lucky to escape alive, according to most of their precepts. Temptation and judgment on sinners were their favorite themes.

In the nineteenth century the climate shifted somewhat. The child was not now primarily a young rascal who must be snatched from the devil's den, but a pupil who must be taught. The schoolteacher—the Sunday-school teacher—is never far from the nineteenth-century children's hymn. Mrs. Alexander, the authoress of "Once in royal David's city" and of "There is a green hill" is very much the schoolteacher. Simplicity is her great virtue: didacticism commonly robs her of that sense of incongruity which delivers the hymn writer from bathos. It was she, after all, who penned the immortal stanza, in a hymn expounding Christian death in terms of the country church graveyard (see Appendix B, pp. 184-85) :

> They do not hear when the great bell
> Is ringing overhead;
> They cannot rise and come to Church
> With us, for they are dead (HAMSt. 575) .

It was therefore not incongruous to cause children to speak of themselves as "little children." This was thought to be a good attitude in a docile pupil.

> We are but little children weak,
> Nor born in any high estate (HAMSt. 331) .

It is interesting then to note that this adjective is applied to the child singer only once in the eighteen hymns in the 1940 Episcopal *Hymnal* (241), and not at all in the ten hymns in the *Pilgrim Hymnal.* And it is further interesting to observe that children's hymns occupy a much smaller proportion of modern books than they formerly did. In England, for example, the *Baptist Hymn Book* (1962) provides twenty-five children's hymns, where its predecessor, the *Baptist Church Hymnal* (1933) gave fifty-eight: and *Congregational Praise* (1951) gives twenty-three where its predecessor, the *Congregational Hymnary* (1916) gave fifty. The Lutheran *Service Book and Hymnal* has no section set apart for children. Neither has the proposed new *Methodist Hymnal,* although it does provide a section of hymns "for Schools and Colleges."

The twentieth century has asserted that children are human beings and should be treated as such, neither insisting on their special propensities to sin nor on their inability to assimilate anything but direct pedagogy. Therefore, in our time hymns for children's praise and worship and hymns embodying images and characters agreeable to the child's outlook have become much more fashionable. A fine example of good doctrine soundly stated is G. W. Briggs's "God my Father, loving me" (H. 239), a hymn which its author was often heard to disparage in later years, but which nonetheless does excellent service (see Appendix B, p. 185). Percy Dearmer was always good in this field: his "Remember all the people" (H. 262, P. 484) is a good example of the picturesque and relevant imagery he was fond of; "Jesus, good above all other" (H. 322) and "Can you count the stars?" (translation: H. 245) are equally good. The most original in common use—and would that there were many more in the same style—is "I sing a song of the saints of God" (H. 243, P. 481), a hymn which, since it was first wedded with the tune in the Episcopal *Hymnal* of 1940 has become very popular in Britain through its use in broadcasting (see Appendix B, pp. 185-86). Hymns that mention "trains" and "tea" as this one does are not often to be found, but their appeal to the youthful mind is irresistible.

Experimental writing for children seems to have made a more vigorous impact on the standard hymnals in Britain than in America. Even where the experiments may be judged unsuccessful it is pleasant to record some reaction against the ponderous didacticism of the nineteenth century. The centers of these experiments were in three hymnals all published in the same year—1925: *Songs of Praise, School Worship,* and *The Church and School Hymnal.* These were all in their various ways reactions against the orthodoxy of the *Sunday School Hymnal* and the Anglican "children's sections" in hymnals current at the time.

79

Even though some of what follows may be quite strange to many readers, it is worth mentioning in order to show what can be done by the bolder spirits.

Songs of Praise really came into its own with the celebrated enlarged edition of 1931, designed for churches and schools that were looking for experiment. It was almost certainly, in that form, the first hymnbook to be used concurrently in Anglican and non-Anglican churches in Britain as the regular manual of praise.[2] Much of its words and music had the school assembly for daily prayers in mind, and many tunes were arranged for piano rather than organ. In its first edition it included a fairly conventional children's section of twenty hymns; but in the later edition seven of these were transferred to the general sections and three were dropped altogether.

The proportion of children's hymns specifically set apart remains about the same: 20 out of 470 in the earlier edition, 29 out of 703 in the later. But the most important development is in the kind of new hymn for children that its editors looked for. Percy Dearmer himself (the editor) wrote many, of which we have mentioned two. But his chief discovery was Jan Struther, an authoress who became famous for the original of a once-celebrated film, *Mrs. Miniver*. Two things proved to be unusual at that date (1931) in her writing: the use of "you" in addressing the Deity, and a development of the imagery of medieval chivalry.

The use of the second person pronoun in prayers and hymns still comes as a shock to many—a shock more profound than the use of many bold images. We hear a little more of it now, even in public worship, in Britain. It is in itself an image—or at least a powerful suggestion—a suggestion of friendship and familiarity which at once pleases some and offends others. It is difficult to see how its intention can be judged otherwise than as following the teaching of the Gospels that a man may address God as his Father; but controversy still continues on the question whether this form can properly be used in ceremonious worship. However, the reaction in children's hymn writing was precisely against the stiff and ceremonious: and in

---

[2] It was, for example, used concurrently in St. Martin's-in-the-Fields, a famous London parish church, and in the Congregational church at Penge, Surrey.

consequence we get this kind of free-ranging imagery, familiar suggestion, and unceremonious address:

> We thank you, Lord of Heaven,
> For all the joys that greet us,
> For all that you have given
> To help us and delight us
> In earth and sky and seas;
> The sunlight on the meadows,
> The rainbow's fleeting wonder,
> The clouds with cooling shadows,
> The stars that shine in splendour—
> We thank you, Lord, for these.
>
> For swift and gallant horses,
> For lambs in pastures springing,
> For dogs with friendly faces,
> For birds with music thronging
> Their chantries in the trees;
> For herbs to cool our fever,
> For flowers of field and garden,
> For bees among the clover
> With stolen sweetness laden—
> We thank you, Lord, for these (SP. 692).

As a literary composition this is at least elegant, and as a protest against stiffness it is significant. It even protests against the tyranny of direct rhyme, using, except between lines 5 and 10 of each stanza, assonance. (If any writer, by the way, thinks this is easier to do than direct rhyme, let him try his hand!) On the other hand, it could be criticized as being somewhat naturalistic and in a sophisticated sense "countrified"; it is still not possible, any more than it was in the days of "All things bright and beautiful," to thank God for the pleasures of urban life. "Homely dwelling-places" in the only other verse is the nearest we get to that. Mannered? Perhaps. Somewhat fanciful? Yes. But in 1931 it was a considerable gesture.

The other well-known hymn (in Britain) of Jan Struther's has the following opening verse:

When a knight won his spurs, in the stories of old,
He was gentle and brave, he was gallant and bold;
With a shield on his arm and a lance in his hand
For God and for valour he rode through the land (SP. 377).

That has become very popular with young children in Britain, through its being set to the pleasant carol tune otherwise associated with "How far is it to Bethlehem?" The trouble is, of course, that the romantic view of medieval chivalry died with Alfred Tennyson (and that man of might, Mark Twain, in one of his less successful books, contributed something to its death). Any grown-up with any sense of history knows that this is an extraordinary generalization about the medieval barons, who were as likely to be men of acquisitive temper and arrogant morals as "gentle and gallant." The grown-ups know it: ought we to let the children believe otherwise because there are some edifying stories associated with King Arthur? Does poetic license here claim too much?

Congregations in the United States are unlikely to be faced with this problem: perhaps it will come when somebody begins to romanticize the Pilgrim Fathers in hymnody. The connection between chivalry and the faith comes, of course, through a transference from the Pauline image of the "Soldier of Christ," which must engage our attention in a moment. The first children's hymn to employ it was not this of Jan Struther's but "Forth rode the knights of old" (CP. 533), by a Baptist, Vera Walker, who wrote it to illustrate a series of Sunday-school lessons based on a book by Basil Mathews, *The Glorious Quest:* which was itself a typically romantic interpretation of the "crusading" spirit and ethos by a devoted missionary of the older school.

That romance and aspiration do appeal to the young mind is beyond any doubt. For romance (as I have elsewhere remarked) the Christian faith substitutes eschatology. But is this too hard a doctrine for application to ten-year-old Christians? Can we use fairies and goblins in hymnody, and use knights as a kind of good fairy? If children think of Jesus as a kind of good fairy, is their faith damaged? At present on the whole we think it is; and the deadpan realism of the trains and tea in "*I* sing a song of the saints of God," is a striking reaction from this. Even more so is a remarkable hymn in the Methodist *School Hymn Book* (261) which, perhaps uniquely, celebrates urban pleasures. Its first line is "Come, let us remember the joys of the town," and among other things we meet on the way are "gay vans and bright buses," and "hooters and hammers and whistles and bells." Its author, Miss Doris Gill, wrote it for a special occasion, and it was included in this young people's hymnal: but, as she has been the first to admit, there is a danger, when one deals with urban things, that, unlike trees and rivers of the countryside, they may be swiftly overtaken by obsolescence. In this hymn are "street lamps that twinkle," and engines that "pant": but now street lamps shed a fluorescent blush or a sodium glare: and the panting steam engine has given way to the snorting diesel. The hymn is none the less a brave and cheerful lyric that suggests a commendably realistic attitude to the experience of town children.

The note of chivalry was often struck in the hymns in *School Worship;* this book reacted against the somewhat archaic piety of Carey Bonner's *Sunday School Hymnal* (1905)—very much used in non-Anglican Sunday schools at the time—by emphasizing a somewhat naïve—some might say Pelagian—"strength and joy" motif. But this kind of thing could make a mark in a child's mind:

> Christ rides to the holy war again,
> Leading His own to a new campaign;
> For love of God and for love of man,
> Who will be with Him and lead the van?

[That final word will hardly do now, and within its author's lifetime could raise a giggle among children to whom it represented a strictly contemporary and urban image.]

> For Christ is out, and He turns not back,
> Though fierce the war, and though long the track,
> Till He makes an end of want and woe;
> Who, then, is ready with Him to go?
>
> (MSHB. 310, sts. 1, 5).

Here is another example of the same motif by A. Norman Rowland.

> We're told of one whose eyes flamed war
>   When right was worsted,
> Who though it brought him many a scar
>   For honour thirsted.
> Though life be long, through all its length
> I would love Jesus with my strength.
>
> We're dear to one whose look of love
>   Made hearts beat faster,
> Who raised the troubled soul above
>   His life's disaster.
> Till time and thought and power depart
> I would love Jesus with my heart.

Service of the "crusading" sort appeals to children and is the moving spirit of most uniformed organizations for boys and girls. And it was certainly one of the great achievements of the liberal movement in theology that it loosened the ties between children's instruction and a frowning or pedagogic dogmatism, and responded more willingly than a previous generation had done to the announcements of the psychologists. Children's hymns of this kind were commonly written by clergy and laymen of pronounced social views and of tenuous theological conviction. The values they express are humanist rather than overtly Christian: but the psychologist may well urge us to consider whether the profoundest images of Christian mythology are apprehensible at all by the child's mind. It is for this reason, indeed, that some people (with whom your present author associates himself) are disposed to recommend for children and young people certain imaginative hymns which a full apprehension of Christian theology would view with impatience. There is no doubt that "City of God," for example, is both popular and edifying among school children and young adolescents, and while its theological unsureness arouses the contempt of the theologically educated, there may be a case of its use among those who are gladdened by its large images.

The attraction of the large and magnificent for the young mind is a matter which the sophisticated and blasé seniors ought to view with greater sympathy. For the full-grown, the magnificence is all reserved for the passion and resurrection of Christ, for the great design of God in creation, redemption, and justification. It is a fact which, whether we care for it or not, we must live with, that many are brought to this wonder at God's grace through the cultivation of the faculty of wonder at a lower level: and many are brought to the joy of Christ's service through the arousing of their aspiration to service at a human level. The delusiveness of "chivalry" probably takes imagination too far off the straight road: but healthy ambition to serve not as a slave or a scullion but as a soldier or at least a Boy Scout is certainly not out of place in children's hymns.

The most experimental children's writer of all, however, was J. M. C. Crum, whose work was chiefly publicized in *The Church and School Hymnal*. Crum did not at all ally himself with the urban realists. It was "England's green and pleasant land" for him. His two favorite themes were the lesson of Matt. 6:24 ff. about the carefreeness of the flowers and birds and the duty of young people to make their country gracious. The second of these is illustrated in such a verse as this, which shows the tenderness of his style—a tenderness which was sometimes perilously near sentimentality:

> Let us pray the Christ that he would make us soldiers,
>   Truer in his ways and braver in his fight:
> That we, as they, may loyally obey,
>   And help to make our England
>   A happy, lovely England,
> Happy in his praise and lovely in his light
>   (HAMR. 455, st. 3).

And here are two verses from a hymn on Matt. 6:24 ff. which again show his whimsical style:

> O man what troubled thoughts you think,
>   How anxious is your care!
> What shall we eat? what shall we drink?
>   And what shall we have to wear?
> As tho' the Father who gave you life
>   Forgot that you were there.
>
> The poppy unpacks her little green box,
>   And her scarlet is outspread;

> She has woven her silk without a loom,
> And sewn it without a thread;
> Lovelier dresses than any princess's:
> How soon are her petals shed! (SSP. 438, sts. 1, 3.)

(The "lilies" of Matt. 6:29 may well have been poppies, according the commentators.) That may easily be Canon Crum's best hymn, although many others are excellent poetry.[3] It is at least a kindly gesture to make contact with a child's imagination by thus expanding on "Consider the lilies."

Now to return to the main theme of this chapter: this excursus on children's hymns is designed to show what it means to "discover as we read." It is in the child's mind that images make their deepest impact. Fully grown Christians are better translators, as it were, and are liable always to make the mistake that C. S. Lewis mentioned, of saying "the valley means humility" or "the soldier means the active Christian." The child, until he has been made sophisticated by his education, will never do this. He will let his mind be crowded with pictures, and will in a few years be saying, in effect, "The Christian life is like this picture, and that picture: like the innocent glory of flowers or the energy and purposefulness of crusaders."

There is just one large psychological question whose answer we must agree on before we can creatively judge the value of imagery in children's hymns—or in any hymns that use it powerfully. Too few people are prepared to make up their minds on the real meaning of "except ye be as little children" (Matt. 18:3). One answer, obviously wrong, still has much currency. This is the assumption that in order to "enter the kingdom" one must remain naïve and untouched by the values of the adult world. To insist on this for oneself is to cultivate infantilism, and infantilism is one of the church's worst enemies. "I'm a simple fellow: don't trouble me with those subtleties" is not a Christian attitude. On the contrary, it directly contradicts the real teaching of Matt. 18:3. The child is not praised because he has not grown up: he will not be further praised if he

---

[3] See also "To God who makes all lovely things" (CP. 41) and his most remarkable essay in hymnic humor, No. 277 in the *Church and School Hymnal*, quoted in my own *Hymns and Human Life* (London: John Murray Ltd., 1952), p. 258.

remains a child. He is praised because of the qualities that belong to childhood and which ought to endure into adulthood. These qualities do not include physical smallness or mental immaturity, but they do include courage, adventurousness, and the longing to learn.

There is a profound difference between wanting to let children be children and wanting to keep them children. The eighteenth-century writers did not care for children as children, being too anxious for them to grow up. The nineteenth-century writers tended to shelter them in a religious enclave, an enclave as jolly and exciting, to be sure, as a tent in the backyard, but still one in which they must remain for as long as they can be persuaded to stay. The twentieth-century writers have made some effort to treat children as children: but the danger is that they will even more than the nineteenth-century writers romanticize childhood and let the children think that nothing lies beyond what they can assimilate at the age of thirteen. Constantly seeds must fall into the ground and die. Before I have done I hope to drive home this particular doctrine concerning hymns—that a large number of them are meant to be used and discarded, that few of them are meant to be part of a Christian's permanent equipment. Children's hymns are especially of this kind.

Soldiers

We have already made some reference to the image of the soldier, and this is the point where it can relevantly be considered. Its most famous employment is in Charles Wesley's "Soldiers of Christ, arise" (H. 552, P. 384, M. 282, MR.). That hymn is a paraphrase and expansion of Eph. 6:10 ff. A more popular, less profound hymn on the "soldier" theme is "Onward, Christian soldiers" (H. 557, P. 382, M. 280, MR.).

In the days of the apostolic writings a soldier was a familiar sight. He was, among other things, what a policeman is today. He was a symbol not only of the defense of the country from enemies, but of the preservation of civic order. But also, in those days, he was bound to be, whatever his nationality, in the employment of Rome. This would be true whether he were stationed in Jerusalem or in that district of southern Turkey to which Ephesians was written. In this passage of Scripture the point is that as a soldier is well equipped for his work by clothing and instruments provided for him by his employer, so the Christian is equipped for his work by gifts provided by God. The allegory would at once make contact with the reader's experience.

Nowadays, what do we really think of when we sing "Soldiers of Christ," or "Onward, Christian soldiers"? We think of this ancient functionary, dressed in armor. Elsewhere [4] I have attempted a remythologization of the images in this passage in terms of what was at the time a historic event in the minds of my English readers —the ascent and conquest of Mount Everest. I there ventured to substitute the climber's equipment for that of the ancient soldier.

That is no longer a topical image (unless perhaps the remarkable interest in the popularity of small-scale mountaineering in Britain may keep it alive for awhile). But something of the kind can serve to show how differently we think of the Christian life when we see it this way, from when we see it in terms of a soldier who is part of remote history and, in any case, engaged in keeping order. The soldier in armor is picturesque: the soldier-scientist of modern times isn't even that.

He is irrelevant, of course, because we think differently now about war from the way the early Christians thought, or even from the way everybody thought when "Onward, Christian soldiers" was written in 1865. True, it is written elsewhere that our enemy is not flesh and blood but principalities and powers: but so often these spiritual things are clothed in human bodies and appropriated by human minds, and the shame and terror of open international conflict are now so evident to us as to obliterate altogether the sense of honor and adventure which until 1916 went with the idea of warfare.

The situation is further complicated by the quite legitimate question, How proper is it to speak of the church as an "army"?

> Like a mighty army
> Moves the Church of God (H. 557).

Thus in "Onward, Christian soldiers," or in Charles Wesley's well-known hymn of the church triumphant:

[4] *Hymns and the Faith,* p. 201.

> One army of the living God
> To His command we bow (M. 422, MR.).

Timothy, in the New Testament, is exhorted to be a "good soldier of Christ," but the extension of "army" for "church" is not so firmly grounded in Scripture. It is romantic to think that the church has the unity, and dubiously edifying to think it has the traditional blind discipline, of an army.

This allegory, then, has the effect of inducing a romantic and aspiring idea of the church which may well be an incentive to adolescent religion. But a faith which is both contemporary and adult will be impatient of any naïveté in the imagery. Perhaps it will be best satisfied with the new dimension given to the "army" idea of the church in James Montgomery's superb hymn, "Lift up your heads, ye gates of brass" (see Appendix B, pp. 186-87):

> Ye armies of the living God,
> Ye warrior's of Christ's host (L. 308).

The combination of energy and mystery in that hymn, which represents Montgomery at his very greatest, gives it exactly the right emphasis for the church's missionary work; it is surprising that it appears to be so little known in the United States.

But by contrast, it is at least possible that the naïve imagery of "Onward, Christian soldiers" will cause a singer to "discover as he reads," and thereby to develop a settled habit of thinking, that the church is like an army: and this may give him a distorted sense of the doctrine of authority in the church. There is a point of religious development beyond which one does not particularly wish to think of the church as a gang or a collection of hearty and like-minded people: and this point is probably fairly early in one's religious development. It is with some sense of propriety, I feel, that the *Lutheran Hymnal* places this hymn among the "spiritual songs," by which designation it appears to mean "hymns of doubtful doctrine that go to pleasing tunes but should not be taken too seriously." There is a case for such a section of "gang songs" and humanistic carols in any hymnbook. They may be useful at certain points of spiritual education, but their indiscriminate use is dangerous.

89

5. Images
for Today

The Hymn Writer's Present Duty

What kind of language should a modern hymn writer employ if he is to hope to emulate the influence and beneficial power of the classics of the literature? Three things can at once be said.

1. It is the hymn writer's duty to scrutinize with the greatest care the images he uses, the suggestions and hidden assumptions in each word he puts into his line. This is especially his duty today because the literature is now so crowded with familiar hymns which rely on words, images, and thought forms which are of their own age but not of ours. A hymn will not be contemporary if its language is the work of an uncritical imitator of the style of another age.

2. It is further his duty to be so closely in touch with contemporary life and religion as to be able to find new images, or to put old ones to new employment, such as will illuminate the singer and speak to his condition. It is unlikely that a new hymn writer will write well unless he is fairly well read in contemporary literature (including fiction), and unless he has at least had some serious talk with a man of science, supposing that he is not already a man of science himself.

3. It is likely that he will do best if he begins, in these days, from argument rather than from image, building outward from reason rather than inward from imagination.

A Good Modern Example: "O God of earth and altar"

I think that these points are all illustrated initially by reference to a single hymn of our age, G. K. Chesterton's "O God of earth and altar."

> O God of earth and altar,
>   Bow down and hear our cry,
> Our earthly rulers falter,
>   Our people drift and die;
> The walls of gold entomb us,
>   The swords of scorn divide:
> Take not thy thunder from us,
>   But take away our pride.
>
> From all that terror teaches,
>   From lies of tongue and pen,
> From all the easy speeches
>   That comfort cruel men,
> From sale and profanation
>   Of honor and the sword,
> From sleep and from damnation
>   Deliver us, good Lord.
>
> Tie in a living tether
>   The prince and priest and thrall,
> Bind all our lives together,
>   Smite us and save us all;
> In ire and exultation,
>   Aflame with faith, and free,
> Lift up a living nation,
>   A single sword to thee   (H. 521, P. 436).

It is heartening to an Englishman to observe how the necessity of this hymn is now taken for granted in hymnbooks of the United States; this is not yet so in Britain. It will not be found, for example, in the *Methodist Hymn-Book* (1933), or the *Baptist Hymn Book* (1962), both official hymnals of major denominations; and it is not in *Hymns Ancient and Modern* (1950). Its absence from the last named was due to a copyright difficulty: its absence from the first two was, I believe, caused by the words in the second line of the third stanza. American Protestants seem to be less ready to let ecclesiastical sensitiveness deprive them of a noble piece of literature. And it is noble literature! There are many hymns—good but commonplace —whose argument could be summed up in a sentence. But the condensation of so much into twenty-four lines in this hymn is unparalleled in the history of the form. I believe that it illustrates very well our three points, even though it was composed as long ago as 1906.

First of all, it is clearly the work of a writer who has a large vocabulary at his command, and who is never at a loss for precisely the word he wants. The suggestions within the words Chesterton uses here are always precisely what he means, and not suggestions that blur his real meaning. There is a line in Frank Mason North's well-known and poignant hymn, "Where cross the crowded ways of life," which illustrates the opposite process:

> From tender childhood's helplessness,
> From woman's grief, man's burdened toil,
> From famished souls, from sorrows' stress
> Thy heart has never known recoil (M. 465, st. 3, MR.) .

The rest of this hymn is so closely argued and carefully written that the reader is apt to ask whether the author really meant us to gather that grief is the woman's lot and burdened toil the man's, in the society of his time. The antithesis is a false and contrived one. In a general way one agrees, and one can allow that pedantry carried to this length is unnecessary. But what gives Chesterton distinction is that in his lines there is no point where, if you apply pressure, the structure even begins to sag.

It is no accident, of course, that in anything so tautly written there are few adjectives. This is a full list of them: *earthly, easy, cruel, living, living, single.* When every adjective will stand pressure, the writing is strong. Each adjective is in implied antithesis with another. "Earthly" is contrasted with the whole idea of God's almightiness: "easy" is directly related with "cruel." The first "living" is contrasted with the "deadness" of the nexus of fear referred to in the previous stanza. The second "living" consciously picks up the first one, and "single" directly contradicts the idea of confusion which was suggested in the vivid verb "drift" in the first stanza.

It used to be said that the marker of a certain aristocratic but now defunct English motorcycle would boast that if you lifted one of his motorcycles on a crane by its headlamp, the structure would not be damaged. Writing like this is of the same homogeneous kind. Wherever you touch it, it is alive, and the connection with the rest is entirely established and indestructible.

Now the author of these lines was, when he wrote them, a lapsed English nonconformist. Sixteen years later he became a Roman Catholic, but in 1906 Chesterton was a profoundly religious person who had largely cut himself adrift from that section of English religion from which hymns tended to come. He was a poet in his own right, and already an accomplished and celebrated writer (though he was but thirty-two years old). The striking quality in his writing is how very little it owes in outward form to the Bible. This is a point which we have met before and which I propose to take up again; here I only say, in anticipation of a later argument, that we have probably been badly misled by those who have told us (and I admit that I have in my younger days subscribed to this teaching) that biblical language is of the *esse* of hymn writing. Chesterton, anyhow, has been able to combine lyricism with freshness, and to produce a hymn which in no respect offends against doctrine (although it may offend susceptibilities). It is entirely delivered from religious catch phrases. Frank Mason North was not entirely delivered from them:

> Yet long these multitudes to see
> The sweet compassion of thy face (M. 465, st. 4, ll. 3-4, MR.).

"Sweet" is an uncritical word. Chesterton would not have written it in that context.

Secondly, there is every evidence here that Chesterton was closely in touch with the inner forces of social life in his time. His hymn is, of course, on the subject of politics: and it may be remarked that some of the best literature in hymns is on this subject just because it has come comparatively recently into the currency of hymnody.

This sympathy with the real need of his time has caused him to talk not of grief so much as greed, not of pain so much as fear. His experience as a political commentator caused him to see the mischief done by "the easy speeches that comfort cruel men."

It is, indeed, the only hymn which exclusively deals with politics in terms of sin and wickedness and confession, and not at all in terms of sorrow and healing. It may also be observed how Chesterton uses words in a strictly contemporary sense. He is at heart a militant medievalist—hence his insistence on "sword" (one of his favorite words in all his writings) : but he is also a modern, for none of any other age could have put quite this sense into the word "drift." And none of any other age would have thought of writing "lies of tongue *and pen*." Chesterton was a newspaperman and knew what the pen had lately found itself able to do in the way of corrupting men's minds.

Thirdly, it is yet clear that this hymn was built outward from argument rather than inward from image. It is obvious that the writer knew before he began to write exactly what he wanted to say. He wanted to write about aspiration toward a Christian society, and about the special evils which, in his time, impeded progress toward that hope. He especially wanted to write about class contempt ("the swords of scorn") and economic greed ("the walls of gold") and intellectual vileness ("easy speeches" and "lies") ; and he wanted to express the reality of God's judgment and grace ("smite and save") . He wanted to express a hope for peace instead of war between what the Scots call "the three Estates" (prince, priest, thrall). And for his argument he had evidence—evidence that he had observed. It has shown itself to be a valid argument still. Now, more than ever we suffer under lies and intellectual promiscuity, under class-tension (this is especially true in Britain), under perverse economic pressures. The argument is right, so the images take their proper place. And as a matter of fact the images are extremely economically deployed. They are associated here not with large phrases but with single words, and with the juxtaposition of words. The imagination is quickened by a series of unusual and powerful and very simple words—"drift and die," "walls of gold," "swords of scorn," "comfort cruel men," "sleep and damnation," "smite and save"—and of course the author's gift (sometimes affectation) of alliteration adds to the lyric power of these expressions.

Although Chesterton's lines are no nearer perfection than those of any other good hymn (perhaps there is one "sword" too many!); this is still an excellent example of the modern manner of writing.

Social Concerns

Social concerns, we have just said, have produced much good writing. Here are a few other examples.

From Henry Scott Holland's "Judge eternal" (1902):

> Still the weary folk are pining
>> For the hour that brings release,
> And the city's crowded clangor
>> Cries aloud for sin to cease;
> And the homesteads and the woodlands
>> Plead in silence for their peace
>>>> (H. 518, P. 435, st. 3).

From Harry Emerson Fosdick's "God of grace" (1930):

> Cure thy children's warring madness,
>> Bend our pride to thy control;
> Shame our wanton, selfish gladness,
>> Rich in things and poor in soul.
> Grant us wisdom, grant us courage,
>> Lest we miss thy kingdom's goal
>>>> (H. 524, P. 365, st. 3).

From S. C. Lowry's "Son of God, eternal Saviour" (1893):

> By thy patient years of toiling,
>> By thy silent hours of pain,
> Quench our fevered thirst of pleasure,
>> Shame our selfish greed of gain
>>>> (H. 500, P. 413, st. 3, ll. 5-8).

From Laurence Housman's "Father eternal" (1919):

> Envious of heart, blind-eyed, with tongues confounded,
>> Nation by nation still goes unforgiven;
> In wrath and fear, by jealousies surrounded,

> Building proud towers which shall not reach to heaven:
> Thy kingdom come, O Lord, thy will be done
> (H. 532, P. 445, st. 3).

Walter Russell Bowie's "O holy city" (H. 494, P. 420, M. 474, MR.) and "Lord Christ, when first thou cam'st to men" (H. 522, P. 325, MR.) must be regarded as among the very best hymns of politics and prophecy ever written.

But these few examples make more urgent the question we must now ask, which is: How should we expect the modern writer to use his Bible? Is the use of biblical language of the essence of a good hymn?

The Spirit and the Letter

One of the things that is fairly clear about these good modern hymns is that where their argument is good and their imagery well judged, their language is usually singularly unlike the biblical cadence of the classic hymn writers. In Isaac Watts and Charles Wesley, in Philip Doddridge and Augustus Toplady at their best, in James Montgomery always and in the best of Thomas Kelly and Eustace Conder, the power of the language is in its biblical rhythm, its direct reminiscence of the King James Version.

> Forbid it, Lord, that I should boast,
> Save in the death of Christ, my God;
> All the vain things that charm most,
> I sacrifice them to his blood (H. 337, P. 198).

Those lines would be grotesque if they did not recall at once to us the profound thought and the dramatic context of Gal. 6:14.

Now, with all the familiar cadences of the great classic hymns ringing in our ears, let us attend to certain harsh words recently set down by a truculent Scottish atheist poet, Hugh MacDiarmid. They come from a lecture delivered in 1961 on the philosopher David Hume. I propose to quote an extended passage from it, since a short quotation will hardly give the reader time to get over the shock of reading such outspoken words. MacDiarmid is pleading for intellectual chastity and sees in conventional Christian speech a primary agent of intellectual promiscuity. As an example of its corrupting influence he cites John Ruskin; and as the chief instrument of this corruption he mentions the Bible. Having spoken of a gesture he made, in some hope of a new secularized society, forty years before, he goes on:

Since then religion has by the most unscrupulous means staged a very considerable come-back—in influence if not in church membership. We had gone a long way prior to the first World War to secure a secularised educational system. No so-called religious instruction has invaded our schools very strongly again. We have industrial chaplains and the horrors of the Tell Scotland Movement and a readiness to lower standards to any depth to welcome an abomination like Billy Graham, as if the dire results of the never-to-be-forgotten Moody and Sankey campaign were not still confining a large proportion of our people in a ghastly rut.

I am opposed to Sunday schools—and religious instruction in day-schools—for the same reason that I am opposed to brain-washing or to the hidden persuaders and subliminal propaganda. The great obstacle to the spread of Human ideas and to intellectual and aesthetic development in Scotland generally can be exemplified in what happened to the genius of one great Scotsman . . . I refer to John Ruskin: and Mr. R. H. Wilenski said that Ruskin largely failed in his life's endeavours for the simple reason that he could not write. . . . It is, I think, accurate to say that he could not write, because all through the years of his maximum activity he was incapable of using language as a precise means of communicating ordered thought. . . . The trouble was that he was a victim of a vice. He was addicted from childhood to a drug which he was forced to take in daily doses in the nursery until he acquired the taste for it. In youth and maturity he fought against the abuse of the drug, but he fought in vain; when at last he was immuned by satiety, his power of action was all spent.

The drug, of course, was the language of the Bible. Ruskin, as everyone knows, was made to read the Bible *aloud* every day in childhood and early youth. . . . He was also made to memorize long sections of the text. . . . He continued to read the Bible as long as he read anything. He was always obsessed with the emotive rhythm, the sonority, the obscurity, the archaism, and awful associations of this living text within his brain. . . . The remembered language continually intervened between the thought and its expression, and often side-tracked the thought itself . . . Again and again a paragraph begins as precise writing and ends as emotive rhetoric recalling the Bible. In book after book the words on the first page . . . submissively obey the thought; then gradually

97

the words become more biblical, and so emotive, till, in the end, the thought is dancing to their tune. . . .

Despite the vast sums we spend on education to-day, and the emphasis publicly placed on the importance of science, we allow thousands of ministers, themselves addicts of the same mass drug, to contaminate the minds of their hearers Sunday after Sunday.[1]

Allowing as much as you please for the gross and arrogant misunderstanding of Christianity, the unscrupulous confusion of Christianity with its expression by one class of Christians, which vitiates much of what MacDiarmid says, there is no way of briefly or facilely answering what he says about the emotive language of the Bible as a disincentive to clear thought.

This is something that must now be boldly faced by Christians. And our argument will proceed as follows: (1) the language of the King James Version has certain peculiarities which induce in a modern ear romantic rather than truthful reactions; (2) the situation is now radically altered, and much for the better, by the increasing use of modern translations; and (3) the greatest hymn writers have always seen the real implications of this.

The Delusive Beauty of the Bible

The peculiar rhythm and cadence of the King James Version has one single and simple cause: the fact that it is a very close, almost pedantic, rendering of the original Hebrew and Greek, promoted by scholarly and devout Puritans who reverenced the text of the Scriptures as sacred in itself. In the English versions for a long time any word not actually representing a word in the original language was printed in italic.

It must be noted at once that the language of the King James Version is not the language of early seventeenth-century English speech or writing. This has been admirably demonstrated by C. S. Lewis in his lecture, *The Literary Impact of the Authorized Version,* and I have myself referred to it elsewhere in another context.[2]

[1] Hugh MacDiarmid, *David Hume, Scotland's Greatest Son* (Edinburgh: the Paperback Booksellers, 1961) , pp. 9-11. Used by permission.
[2] *English Religious Dissent* (London: Cambridge University Press, 1960) .

Elizabethan Englishmen did not speak in parallel clauses such as one constantly encounters in the Old Testament, or in sentences constantly beginning with "And," which the gospels provide long series together. From the beginning this was "odd" English, and from the beginning it was able to gather round itself an atmosphere of "separateness." Since the "sacred" is by derivation and ancient association the "separate," the "sacredness" of the Scriptures could be easily taken by the unwary to reside in its peculiar and haunting rhythm and cadence. Therefore, to say something in scriptural rhythm, whether or not Scripture is accurately quoted, is to give that statement a certain a priori authority and status. And by transference, even a misquotation of Scripture can come to have status if the rhythm is sufficiently reminiscent of that of the King James translation of the sacred book.

The connection between this and the peculiarly English (or at least English-speaking) habit of fundamentalism is obvious. When we compare the linguistic status of the English Bible of 1611 with that of Luther's translation of the German Bible, we are also comparing attitudes toward the Bible in the two cultures. Luther's Bible founded the German language of literature and speech. King James's Bible set itself apart in a linguistic enclave from the start. So if there is a German fundamentalism it tends to be a fundamentalism of dogma rather than of the letter: and where English-speaking fundamentalism flourishes, it flourishes as a fundamentalism of the letter, even of the letter of an English translation whose fallibility is demonstrable and whose linguistic oddness is evident to anybody who has read any seventeenth-century prose.

Here are two examples of the hidden persuasion in the language of the King James Bible having curious consequences. There is a prayer which is ascribed to Ignatius of Loyola, and which is very much used in schools, student societies, and found in every anthology of prayers. It begins, "Teach us, Good Lord, to serve thee as thou deservest," and contains the phrase, "To give, and not to count the cost." Now this English version of Loyola's expresses an admirable sentiment: but it recalls at once a statement in the Gospels that uses the same words, but that actually states the opposite moral principle from that stated in the prayer:

99

54169

For which of you, intending to build a tower, sitteth not down first, and counteth the cost, whether he have sufficient to finish it? Lest haply, after he hath laid the foundation, and is not able to finish it, all that behold it begin to mock him, saying, This man began to build, and was not able to finish (Luke 14:28-30).

The telling phrase in both passages is "count the cost"—alliterative and epigrammatic and very slightly odd (therefore "sacred") English. But the teaching of the parable is that one should count the cost of an enterprise: that of the prayer is that one should not. But nine Christians out of ten who hear that prayer believe that the teaching of Jesus was that the cost should not be counted.

There is a similar example of double-talk in no less august a source than Charles Wesley. In a hymn beginning "For ever here my rest shall be" he wrote:

> Wash me, and make me thus Thine own,
> Wash me, and mine Thou art;
> Wash me, and not my feet alone,
> My hands, my head, my heart (MHB. 456, st. 3).

In a characteristic way he leaps from Psalm 51 to John 13; but unhappily he obscures the point that when Peter said, "Lord, not my feet only, but also my hands and my head," he was rebuked by the Master for misunderstanding the significance of the washing of the disciples' feet.

In yet another context, I recall seeing, every time I dined in the Hall of Mansfield College, Oxford, an inscription over the fireplace, placed there, it is believed, by the suggestion of the first principal, A. M. Fairbairn. It shows the Latin version of the text, "Blessed is he that shall eat bread in the kingdom of God" (Luke 14:15). But the context of that quotation shows it to have been a sentimental comment by somebody present when our Lord was speaking of the hospitality of the kingdom, to which the Master replied with a parable that both exposed and denounced his misunderstanding of what Jesus was saying.

Returning to hymns, what is one to say of these familiar lines, which I am relieved to find are not considered indispensable in their native America, but which can be found in the *Pilgrim Hymnal.*

> Not for-ever in green pastures
> Do we ask our way to be,
> But the steep and rugged pathway
> May we tread rejoicingly.
>
> Not for-ever by still waters
> Would we idly rest and stay,
> But would smite the living fountains
> From the rocks along our way (P. 368, sts. 2-3).

That is almost excellent, but in fact banal: it is an attempt to contrast the life of Christian energy with that of quietistic sloth. The contrast in the second quatrain of the still waters with the springs that recall the exodus is in itself brilliantly witty: but it is outrageous to achieve this stroke of wit by suggesting that the twenty-third Psalm is a psalm for sluggards. And in using the expressions "still waters" and "green pastures," that is what the author does (see Appendix B, p. 187). The language of the King James Version can be inspiring, but to the unwary it can be a seduction from clear thought. Stray quotations from it are not given the status of sacredness where they have the effect of sidetracking the thought of the reader from the truth with which their context is concerned.

The Modern Bibles

A new situation in hymn writing is certainly brought about by the radical reformation in semantics that has been associated with the widespread use of modern translations—Weymouth, Moffatt, Goodspeed, the Revised Standard Version, the New English Bible. These are nowadays liable to be in many pulpits and many homes. The appearance of these new translations has, and it is no accident, coincided with an age in which those social habits which caused John Ruskin to be obliged to read the Bible aloud every day have passed away. The private reading of the Scriptures still continues: but the family reading has largely disappeared: the reading *aloud,* which caused the especially aural qualities of the text to have such powerful effect, has gone. While many regret this, there is substance in MacDiarmid's implied satisfaction in it, for if the once-familiar cadences are no longer familiar, then the mental seduction they exercised will lose its influence.

The advent of the new translations in itself represents a consciousness of the need for the Bible to be directly intelligible rather than piously but approximately intelligible. It recognizes the need to say without shame that the King James Version is usually beautiful but not always understandable. And while there is no lover of the Scriptures who has not felt that a modern translation has ruined one of his favorite passages, sentimental attachment to the *sound* of a passage must never be allowed to dictate to the mind's ability to understand its meaning as nearly as it can.

What will the acceptance of new translations do to the language of our hymns? It is fair to say, I think, that even if a single new translation were as universally authorized, or as universally viewed with reverence and affection, as the King James has been, it would still never have the effect on the language of hymns that the King James has had: this is partly because reading habits are different nowadays, and the *sound* of the Bible is not now so conspicuous a part of our aural experience as it was for Protestants between 1611 and 1900. But it is partly also because of a change in the habits of translators: for it is now regarded as proper to translate into idiomatic English, rather than to translate word by word as the Puritan translators did. This brings the language of the Bible nearer to the language of ordinary literature (or in some cases, as in the work of J. B. Phillips, to the language of common life), and thereby removes the "sacred separateness" which made the original memorable —and made it dangerous.

The Real Implications

The consequence of this is bound to be that hymn writers, if they wish to be scriptural, will now be able to achieve this only by being faithful to the underlying ideas, dogmas, and patterns of the Scriptures. They will no longer be able to appear scriptural by using direct verbal reminiscences.

This is, I contend, what has already begun to happen, and had begun to happen before the age of new vernacular translations had really opened. The new criterion of scriptural faithfulness will not be how much actual scriptural sound the words make, or even how many images are directly derived from the Scriptures, but how far the argument of the Scriptures is preserved.

Now in Laurence Housman's hymn "Father Eternal" (H. 532, P. 445) quoted on pages 95-96, it would be possible to say that scriptural image and scriptural thought are both preserved and very beautifully used. The image of Babel and that of the birth at Bethlehem are brought into powerful juxtaposition. But further— and this is to apply the modern criterion—the total thought expressed in the hymn is at no point in discord with the total teaching of Christ about politics. The simplest categories are employed— humility and compassion—and it was always the breach of these which Jesus criticized in contemporary Jerusalem. Similarly Chesterton's lines are conformable with the Scriptures, although they evoke no scriptural language or even images. They are exactly what the Old Testament prophets tended to say about the conditions of the societies in which they moved: they reflect faithfully the words of such as Samuel, Isaiah the first, and Amos. The more one reads those prophets, the closer one finds that Chesterton comes to their thought form.

On the other hand, James Russell Lowell's lines beginning "Once to every man and nation" (H. 519, P. 441), though resonant, probably fail this particular test. Exactly what is meant by "God's new Messiah," whether the crucifixion is adequately described as Christ "standing for truth," whether the lonely martyr guided by his conscience against the whole world is to be identified with Christ and made a figure whom all should admire and imitate—all this is entirely debatable. Lowell's lines seem, therefore, to be an expression of personal opinion in support of a debating point rather than a hymn enshrining timeless doctrine.

The application of this rule of scriptural faithfulness is liable to lead to much difficulty and controversy; there will be some, perhaps, who think Lowell more faithful than Chesterton to the spirit of the Scriptures. All that can be said is that Scripture and creed and church teaching will make excellent hymns if they are clothed with real poetry and worked out with honest precision. What comes of a detachment from doctrine as well as Scripture will possibly be good verse, but it will fall outside the definition of a hymn because of its lack of contact with the objective reality which Christians claim to preach.

This can, however, be reinforced by once again referring to the masters of the eighteenth century. They were scriptural in the old-fashioned way: but the truth is that their best moments came, and their most enduring hymns were written, when they interpreted the spirit as well as the letter of Scripture. "Love divine, all loves excelling" (H. 479, P. 228) is a case in point. Here the most memorable lines are not scriptural quotations. The first line is an adaptation of Dryden, the last a quotation from Addison; most of the rest is the adaptation to the central theme of scriptural ideas. And the hymn really does illuminate obscure passages like II Cor. 3:18, because we remember its friendly and lyrical argument when we next come to such passages, and it increases our sense of being in touch with them.

The greatest hymn of the "romantic" period—Henry H. Milman's "Ride on!" (H. 64, P. 175) —is another good example of a hymn that is veritably bathed in Scripture, and yet almost entirely free from quotations from Scripture, except for its final line (Rev. 11:17). Nobody could call these lines unscriptural: with them it is the spirit, not the letter.

By contrast, with another romantic hymn writer, Reginald Heber, it was often the letter rather than the spirit. Heber set himself to free hymnody from the bondage of "sacred apartness," and to exalt its status as literature. Unhappily he only too frequently managed to lay hold on the least important part of Scripture's message: indeed, it is difficult to find a hymn of his that refers to Scripture at all without doing this. A notorious example is "By cool Siloam's shady rill" (H. 328), a hymn much loved by Scotsmen for use at baptisms, upon which that great Scottish hymnological scholar, Millar Patrick, observed that "it contains a maximum of misstatement in the minimum of space." The connection between the aqueduct of which Siloam formed a part (John 5:1) and the boyhood of Jesus is obscure: Siloam was rarely cool, and was never shady, and the chance of finding lilies by it in its urban setting was slim. Siloam happens to be one of that minority of Hebrew names which sounds euphonious when transliterated into English: one can find no other reason for Heber's bringing it in at all (see Appendix B, pp. 187-88).

His most celebrated hymn, "Holy, Holy, Holy!" (H. 266, P. 251), can be accused of nothing worse than a somewhat laborious tautology, and a tendency to insist on the reposeful quality of heaven at the expense of that riotous atmosphere which Revelation communicates. "Hosanna to the living Lord!" (H. 318) seems to be little more than an inept and prosy adaptation of a Palm Sunday theme to the private necessities of an individual Christian. (What else can be gathered from "chiefest," that ugly piece of un-English, in the fourth stanza?) Heber is at his best when he is simply writing poetry, as in "I praised the earth" (H. 306) and in those parts of "Brightest and best" (H. 46, P. 126) which do not appear to be addressing a star (see Appendix B, pp. 188-89).

One secret about Charles Wesley is not, I think, very well known; attention was first drawn to it by Henry Bett in *The Hymns of Methodism*,[3] but the theme was somewhat expanded in the *Bulletin of the Hymn Society*, No. 80, 1956. This is that Wesley frequently based his expositions of scripture on the commentary of Matthew Henry. His best-known hymn that is indebted to Matthew Henry (whose massive commentary was published in 1700) is "O thou who camest from above" (H. 463). "A charge to keep I have" (CU. 362) is almost a literal versification of Henry's paragraph on Lev. 26:35; and the hymns beginning "Thy ceaseless, unexhausted love" (MHB. 49) and "Captain of Israel's host" (MHB. 608, MR.) are similarly close paraphrases of the same source. This is a very unusual manner of treating scripture; I cannot recall any other example of a hymn writer taking down a commentary and putting its contents into verse: but then there would appear to be few less promising sources of poetry than the usual modern commentary.

Little more is necessary, I think, to show that the real scriptural principle in good hymn writing is the spirit of Scripture rather than its attractive but sometimes misleading letter. But it seems clear that the modern hymn writer will serve his age best if his argument is clear and religious and based in the truth declared in the Scriptures, and clothed in words and images that declare his contact and compassion with the world in which he lives.

[3] Third Edition; London: The Epworth Press, 1945.

6. The
Choice of Hymns

Practical Limitations

The choice of hymns for public worship will normally lie with the minister whose responsibility it is to offer that service. This is normal procedure; it may sometimes be varied, and variation can be legitimate and occasionally may be desirable. But it is the minister who probably knows more about the principles of liturgy and the special needs of the congregation than anybody else in that place, and therefore it is proper that he should either choose the hymns or guide those who choose them.

What limits his choice? He has before him a book containing five or six hundred hymns and a congregation waiting to sing. Those are the primary limiting factors. Exceptional occasions apart, he must keep within the repertory of his hymnal; and equally, he must know what his people can sing and enjoy singing.

Within that first limiting boundary there is a second line of demarcation: that between what is familiar to his people and what is unfamiliar. At any stage in the life of a hymnal, even when it has been published for twenty years, there are hymns and tunes which the people do not know. He who chooses the hymns must know what these are and act on his knowledge—but we are not, of course, going to say that he should never choose what is not familiar. We say only that he needs to *know* what is not familiar.

It may here be said, to clear the ground, that the unfamiliarity of a tune is a much more important factor than the unfamiliarity of words: and that since this book is not concerned with music, we shall say little more about this particular limitation.

But in this same territory there is yet another boundary which intersects the one which we have already observed: that between what this congregation likes and finds easy and what it dislikes and finds difficult. This too ought to be known to the minister. The pattern formed by these boundaries varies very widely from one region to another and from one church to another. Once again, it is not necessary to urge ministers always to choose what people will find agreeable. It is only necessary to urge them to know what they are doing.

The reader may by now have formed a picture or diagram in his mind of an irregularly shaped area (denoting what is in the hymnal) divided into four sections by two crooked lines: (*a*) what is known and liked; (*b*) what is known but not liked; (*c*) what is unknown but would be found easy; (*d*) what is unknown and would be found difficult. In many churches section (*a*) will amount to something like twenty per cent of the hymns in the book—call it one hundred hymns. In many others section (*c*) is probably larger and section (*d*) smaller than the timid might expect them to be. Those are the two things one can reasonably expect.

The Real Meaning of "I don't like it"

Now it is at once necessary to expand a little on the psychology of the very ambiguous and unhelpful verb in the phrase "I like this and I don't like that." The ability to detect the real meaning of this word is a necessary piece of pastoral equipment.

Ninety-nine times out of a hundred it means, "This is familiar; but that, by its unfamiliarity, has impressed me." The phrase "I don't like it" often translates a psychological resistance to something unfamiliar (something un*like* the hearer) which has produced an ambivalent attitude in the hearer. The unfamiliar is disturbing: it is also attractive. The whole "romantic" movement in literature and art, of course, was an exploitation of this ambivalence. Now anybody who is above the age of ten can remember occasions, especially aesthetic occasions, on which that which at first evoked the response "I don't like it" proved to be something to be treasured—something, indeed, which insisted on being made terms with, and whose memory became sweet instead of bitter because of the experience (in which there *was* bitterness) of coming to terms with it. One is reminded of the boy who had successfully completed an endurance course in an "Outward Bound" school. (This is a British institution, in which the Duke of Edinburgh now takes a keen personal interest, designed to promote character and initiative in young people through subjecting them to such hazards as strenuous mountaineering or trekking for extended periods without any organized arrangements for food and shelter.) Asked whether he had enjoyed the experience, he replied, "Yes, very much, but not at the time."

Now those who have made any progress in aesthetic appreciation know all about this. Their progress is a constant, exodus-like succession of variously bitter experiences whose acceptance makes them sweet and strong. This principle goes to the very heart of the Christian gospel, of course: the pattern of the cross and the resurrection, of "dying daily," in the spiritual life is exactly this, raised to the highest spiritual level. It is part of the rhythm of humanity, and this rhythm is, as it were, in "sympathetic vibration" with the rhythm of God's revealed truth. In the Old Testament (Exodus 33) the principle always was that the glory of God was what a man could not look on and live. In the New Testament "we beheld his glory," but the joy of its acceptance lay on the other side of an experience of unutterable terror, concerning which the man possessed by devils said, "Torment me not."

Here we are working at a much lower spiritual level than that: but that which applies in great things is repeated in the small ones. It not only is no service, it is a positive disservice to any congregation so to order worship that nothing ever happens of which is said "I don't like it." A mature Christian will not say that. He will candidly express his wonder and perhaps his feeling of insecurity and danger when a new experience comes. What matters is to note that when the innocent Christian says, "I don't like it," he means the same thing, but is expressing it in a manner which might mislead his hearer. For if what you give another he dislikes, you may feel you ought at once to withdraw it. But if what you have given another has initiated in him an experience which may lead toward growth and glory, then, provided its initial bitterness is not positively destructive, perhaps it should not be withdrawn. Of course it is always wise to note the difference between medicine and poison, between soap and sulphuric acid.

What then is it that hymns *do* to people? As has been said, what they *do* to people is done very largely through their music, because music has at least two levels at which it can be received. One is the superficial level at which it does its work on all who are not tone-deaf. The other is a deeper and more intelligent and critical level, at which it does its work only on the "musical"—those who understand it as a language. Music is, you could almost say (and it will have to serve here because it is not our subject), "images" to nearly everybody and "concepts" to a minority. Therefore, music goes to almost everybody's affections but not to everybody's reason. And as a consequence of that, most people's reactions are emotional, and they find an adequate expression of them in such a phrase as "I don't like it." But the emotional reaction is not the whole, or the most important part, of the truth about the impact of the music.

With words the pattern is exactly the other way. Take words without music and you find that the great majority of people treat the words as simply expressions of concepts—vehicles of reason. It is a minority who see the images which the words convey. Hence the impatience of the majority with poetry of any sort by itself. The more generally literate a culture becomes, the thicker the traffic in words as the bearers of reason, and the more widespread the impatience with words as image bearers. The middle ages in England were full of popular poetry. The modern age is as full of popular small talk.

This is why in our kind of culture it is really quite difficult to get the ordinary man or woman in a congregation to notice what he or she is singing. Take a hymn and remove its tune: what chance would there be of most people's even giving it a second glance, let alone reading it with such patient understanding that it could do the work its author really meant it to do, each word giving full value in suggestion and illumination? Put the tune back, and if it is a popular one, the hymn will be a success—or so it will appear. But it will succeed only in that a number of people have sung it. What it really was meant to do will very probably not have been done at all. It will have been, so far as the service goes, a "break for music"; and the substitution of "Mary had a little lamb" for "O God, our help in ages past" might go unnoticed.

That is perhaps to say too much: but it might not be too much to say that the substitution of the third verse of "Mary had a little lamb" for the third verse of some hymn which the congregation did not know by rote might at least pass unnoticed by a number of those present.

The Primary Image

This leads to a point which must be added to all that we said in the earlier chapters about the work of images in hymns. What was said there about images in detail was designed to stir up an interest in the words for their own sake. But for most people the detailed images hardly make any impact; yet for such people a well-known hymn has, as it were, an overall image which does come through. This image it normally gathers partly from its tune and partly from its opening line. Ideally, this image should really be a summary of the detailed images that pass before the mind's eye as the hymn is being sung. Sometimes, however, the overall image is quite markedly different from the sum, or common factor, of the detailed images. This can have interesting consequences.

Take for example the hymn "The God of Abraham praise" (H. 285, P. 14). Most Christians know this hymn, and it is hardly ever sung to any but its original tune "Leoni." It presents to any singer a very clear image: it suggests very strongly the somber yet luminous majesty attributed to God in the Old Testament, especially in the early chapters of Exodus. Any Christian, asked without notice what it suggested to him, would, I suspect, say something that amounted to that.

The immediate causes of this reaction are the minor mode of the tune, with its beginning on a low note and its rise through a minor tenth during the first two phrases, and the proper name "Abraham" in the first line.

Now it does not matter what version of the hymn, or what selection of verses, is sung; that is what it will primarily do to people— arouse their sense of the Old Covenant majesty of God. But in American use it turns out that "The God of Abraham praise" is not one hymn but two quite distinct hymns. Number 285 in the

1940 Episcopal *Hymnal* is part of the very long version made by Thomas Olivers, based on an old Jewish doxology. A longer selection appears in the *Service Book and Hymnal*, No. 410. But the *Pilgrim Hymnal*, No. 14, and *The Methodist Hymnal*, No. 5, use a version by Newton Mann and Max Landsberg, and their selection contains three stanzas, compared to the five of the 1940 Episcopal *Hymnal* and the eight of the *Service Book and Hymnal*.

Comparing the two versions we find that the incidental images of the two hymns are quite different. That of Olivers (H. and L.) is a Christianization of the old Jewish hymn, which brings in Christ at an early stage (st. 3 in H., st. 4 in L.). Further, the note of the pilgrimage toward heaven and of faith in the eternal things is heard in the stanza "the goodly land we see" (L., st. 3) and in the other references to the heavenly Zion. The long version in the *Service Book and Hymnal* has a reference to the mysterious sight of the risen Lord bearing the wounds of his crucifixion (L., st. 7). Yet another selection, found in English books, has this quatrain:

> I all on earth forsake—
> Its wisdom, love, and power—
> And Him my only portion make,
> My shield and tower
> (MHB. 21, st. 2; CP. 12, st. 2).

Finally, in the last verse of the Olivers version there is an explicit reference to the Christian doctrine of the Trinity.

The incidental images, therefore, include pilgrimage, faith, the ascension, and the Trinity. None of these is discordant with the overall notion of majesty, and the whole hymn makes an impressive creedal utterance, particularly in the context of the teaching of the Old Testament and its Gospel consummation.

The other version (in P. and M.) says quite different things.

> His spirit floweth free,
> High surging where it will (P. 14, M. 5, st. 2, 11. 1-2)

> He hath eternal life
> Implanted in the soul (P. 14, M. 5, st. 3, 11. 1-2).

111

Clearly those lines were written (and editorially selected) by those to whom the robust and primitive images of the Old Testament seemed too steep for contemporary congregations. For these are substituted certain complimentary remarks about the Deity which cannot possibly be thought an adequate substitute. But their tiresome mediocrity is not here in point. What matters is that the hymn is still to almost all singers "The God of Abraham praise," and it may be suspected that "Abraham" is strong enough to counteract a good deal of the emasculating influence of the images in the Mann-Landsberg version.[1]

The preeminence of the overall image is the reason why so many of the most popular hymns have effective first lines and owe their popularity to that effectiveness. Dozens of examples come to mind—"Rock of ages," "The King of love my shepherd is," "Praise my soul the King of heaven," "Ye holy angels bright," "We plough the fields and scatter." The point can be further made by contrast when one remembers the history of "Hark the herald angels sing." Charles Wesley originally wrote, "Hark how all the welkin rings!" using an already somewhat archaic word in his first line. Martin Madan suggested its alteration to the present form, having a keen eye for the initial image that would hold the singer's attention. A rousing tune, adapted to it a century after it was written, has now placed it in everybody's repertory.

When the 1904 edition of *Hymns Ancient and Modern* appeared, published with the express purpose of paying better service both to scholarship and to good taste in hymnody, the great volume of protest which greeted it, and which ensured that it would be, relatively, a failure as an Anglican hymnal, was headed by those who protested against its return to Wesley's opening line with its "welkin" (HAM. 1904, 62). Two years later *The English Hymnal* showed a better sense of public relations in printing both versions—Wesley's original in thirty-two lines and the popular revision in twenty-four (Nos. 23 and 24) ; but the popular one is sung at least twenty times for every singing of the original.

---

[1] It should be said that the Mann-Landsberg version did not originally begin with the line "The God of Abraham praise" but "Praise to the living God" (see MHB. 15). The retention of Olivers' line was very clearly decided on by editors who wanted to keep the "overall image."

Again, there are many great hymns which do not achieve wide popularity because of a lack of this grip in the first line. An outstanding example is another of Charles Wesley's, "Eternal beam of light divine." Godfrey Sampson judged this the greatest of all Wesley's hymns,[2] and it is difficult to gainsay him. Are not these lines irresistible?

> Thankful I take the cup from Thee,
>   Prepared and mingled by Thy skill,
> Though bitter to the taste it be,
>   Powerful the wounded soul to heal.
>
> Speak to my warring passions, Peace!
>   Say to my trembling heart, Be still!
> Thy power my strength and fortress is,
>   For all things serve Thy sovereign will.
>
> O death! Where is thy sting? Where now
>   Thy boasted victory, O grave?
> Who shall contend with God? Or who
>   Can hurt whom God delights to save?
>
> (MHB. 496, sts. 3-6).

In Britain that hymn is sung only by Methodists and Congregationalists. Baptists, Anglicans, and Presbyterians are strangers to it. Even those interdenominational books, *The BBC Hymn Book* and *Christian Praise,* do not include it. I find it in no United States hymnbook (but my knowledge of them is limited). It is in *The Hymnary* of the United Church of Canada (417), but not in the Baptist version of that hymnary, and not in the *Hymnal* of the Canadian Episcopal Church.

And the reason is surely that its opening line—a perfectly adequate line in itself—gives no hint of the abundant richness that is to follow. It looks as if it is going to be an ordinary hymn of praise, opening with a rather extended vocative. In fact, it is the greatest piece of Christian hymnic writing on the subject of Christian suffering and hope that can be found anywhere.

[2] "The Century of Divine Songs," in *Seven Essays* (Cambridge: The University Press, 1947), p. 216.

113

To return then to our main theme: it is this initial image of which the minister choosing hymns must be aware, as well as being aware of the incidental images that follow. The initial image will tell him what impact the hymn will make on his congregation as a whole. The incidental ones will reinforce the points which he especially wants at that time to emphasize, but on many present they will be lost. That they will be lost is no reason for withdrawing attention from them. Provide an abundant banquet. When the five thousand are fed seven baskets of leavings may remain, but never mind: gather them up and regard none as lost.

The Church Year

If the minister has informed himself on these essential matters, he must then see what help he can get from other sources in making his selections. In those communions which observe the Church Year, he has a legitimate and very useful source of help. In Britain the nonepiscopal communions fifty years ago paid scanty attention to the Church Year. More and more they are coming to recognize the edifying value of this yearly unfolding of the drama of our salvation.

The secret of this edifying value is this: that if a congregation has learned how to plot out the great movement of the Church Year, and learned to expect certain emphases on certain great days, the preaching of the gospel is very greatly helped. Really great preaching is partly achieved by an expectant congregation; and it is easier for people to come to church decently prepared for worship when they have a habitual expectation of what the church will be saying to them on that day.

But this, while making the minister's task easier, does not make it less demanding of responsible discharge. Hymnals nowadays mark out their selections in sections corresponding either to seasons or to doctrines (and of course often these overlap). At present the pattern is grossly distorted by the enormous popularity of Christmas carols, which distends the nativity section out of all proportion to that dealing with the six Sundays of Lent or with the season of the ascension. On the whole the best hymnals contain not too many seasonal hymns (carols apart), and leave plenty of room for the selection of hymns of more general import which nonetheless throw light on the special teaching of the season. Epiphany, for example, may cover five Sundays, and Easter necessarily covers five also. The great seasonal hymns mark out the seasons unambiguously. But while "Songs of praise the angels sang" is a good hymn at any season, how especially effective it is when sung soon after Christmas, when the "Gloria in excelsis" is still ringing in the people's memories (see H. 292, ll. 5-8) .[3]

> Songs of praise the angels sang,
> Heaven with alleluias rang,
> When creation was begun,
> When God spake and it was done.
>
> Songs of praise awoke the morn
> When the Prince of peace was born;
> Songs of praise arose when he
> Captive led captivity.
>
> Heaven and earth must pass away,
> Songs of praise shall crown that day;
> God will make new heavens and earth,
> Songs of praise shall hail their birth (L. 432, sts. 1-3) .

For the same season, "Father eternal, Ruler of creation" (H. 532, P. 445) is eminently suitable (see above, pp. 95-96) .

Similarly the Easter season is the time to sing "Abide with me" (H. 467, P. 209) and "Guide me, O thou great Jehovah" (H. 434, P. 93) , and the Passion season is most appropriate for "According to thy gracious word" (P. 284) which, with its second stanza omitted, can be used otherwise than at Eucharistic services.

But the Church Year is not the only aid the minister can look for in choosing his hymns—and during half of the year he is given little help from that source in any case. He may or may not regard the

---

[3] I am disposed here to repeat what I have written elsewhere: that it seems to me a mistake to set this hymn to an eight-line tune, as H. does; and equally to omit any of its lines as L. does (432) . It is written on a carefully worked out pattern in two large sections of twelve lines each, the first dealing with heavenly praises and the second with the earthly praises which respond to them. It ought, therefore, to be sung in full, and either to a four-line tune or possibly to a twelve-line tune, but I do not know of one.

institution of special Sundays by secular or philanthropic agencies as an assistance; for what my own opinion may be worth, I believe that the incursion into the Church Year of special Sundays is a custom which should not be pressed beyond certain very well defined limits, and which in the English-speaking countries has already gone well beyond them.

The Liturgy

The more familiar guide for the choice of hymns is, of course, the liturgy itself. And here we must distinguish between the kind of choice which will be prompted by different liturgical traditions.

Certain church traditions, of which the Episcopal and the Lutheran are familiar examples, have a highly ordered liturgical tradition. Others have a more "charismatic" liturgy. In all forms of church worship there has been in the past generation a tendency to confusion: but none is without a liturgical principle, however far its adherents may have traveled from it in practice.

The most evident distinction between the two broad types is that where a highly ordered liturgy is used, less hymns are called for than where the liturgy is less predictable and prescribed.

For example, in the *Book of Common Prayer* no provision whatever is made for hymns, except for the singing of the Te Deum at Matins, of the Gloria in Excelsis at the Eucharist, and of "Come, Holy Ghost" at ordinations. Congregational participation is sufficiently provided for in the Psalms, the Creeds, and the Responses. In practice, Episcopal churches always include hymns in public worship, although they are commonly omitted from collegiate worship (in cathedrals and seminaries where the full liturgical life is led) . The more popular the design of the service, the greater the prominence that is given to hymns; so that the ordinary parish church may well adorn a Matins-with-sermon with four hymns (one at the beginning, one after the third collect, one after the state prayers, and one after the sermon) : and I have attended an English parish church where at an evening service there were added to these four a hymn before the Magnificat and two at the Benediction with which the service closed. At a parish Eucharist four or five hymns may be sung. But in the Anglican order the principle is that the liturgy would be complete without any of these hymns, and that they are provided for their popular appeal.

A somewhat similar tradition prevails in the Lutheran Church. In the Eucharist as it is prescribed in the *Lutheran Hymnal* and the *Lutheran Service Book and Hymnal* one hymn only is provided for, and this is to be sung following the Creed. At Matins a hymn is prescribed after the Venite (and in the latter another after the lesson) : at Vespers, after the lesson, or, if there be an address, after the address.

This use reflects an important difference from the Anglican custom. Lutherans, being more specifically heirs of the Reformation, see hymns as primarily illustrations of Creed and Scripture. It would not seem to them fitting to omit them from their liturgies. But their use is still limited to the stated places in the liturgies. In practice it is always possible to add processional and recessional hymns, which are strictly no part of the liturgy.

With these traditions the Reformed tradition of such bodies as the Baptists and Congregationalists of Britain or the United Church of Christ in the United States stand in strong contrast. There has been so much interdenominational fusion in the United States that the contrast will be better brought out if we consider for a moment the kind of service which is held in a fairly normal church of the Reformed tradition in Britain. This will serviceably isolate the special principle we mean to emphasize here.

Hymns in the Free Liturgy

In its purest form the Reformed tradition relies entirely on hymnody for congregational participation in the service. Congregationally spoken or sung responses appear in modern examples of Reformed worship, but they are imported from the Lutheran or Anglican traditions. Moreover, the choir and the anthem are, strictly speaking, importations as well. In the Genevan order of service, on which the usual service in a British Congregational or Baptist Church, or in the Church of Scotland, is founded, no provision is made for a choir separate from the main singing body. Since it is in Scotland that reformed worship persists in the purest form in which it will be found in an English-speaking country, we show here the order of morning worship which is held on a non-Communion Sunday in the Scottish

Congregational church where I myself minister. (Normal Scottish custom celebrates the Communion quarterly, but this church's custom is to celebrate it monthly.)

PRAISE
  Opening Sentences
  Prayers of Invocation and Confession
  Assurance of Pardon
    Brief Address to the Children, with Reading
  PRAISE: "The Lord will come and not be slow" (H. 312, P. 95)
    Prayer with the Children
    The Lord's Prayer Said by All
    Dismissal of the Children [who continue their worship in another part of the building]
  Collection of Offerings
  Intimations [announcements]
  Prayer of dedication of Offerings and Work
PRAISE
  Readings from Scripture [Old Testament, Epistle, Gospel]
PRAISE
  Sermon
  Prayers of Intercession and Thanksgiving
PRAISE
  Blessing

In this church "Praise" means a hymn or a metrical psalm or one of the Scottish paraphrases. It is perhaps more frequently found in Scotland that the intercessions precede the readings: but the Genevan order favors the arrangement above.

Now here we have the merest skeleton of a liturgy. True, the order of service is such that a smooth logical connection is always apparent between the successive movements of the worship. The order is far from ideal: there is one very clear "break," at the point where the children leave the church and the taking of the offering follows. This is in itself an unhappy incursion into the service, although the association of domestic intimations with the collection, and the dedication not only of the specific monetary gifts but of the lives from which they come, has a clear significance. But it is a fair example of the approach towards Reformed custom that is still made in this kind of church. And everything depends on the hymns.

That is to say, if the hymns here are not chosen with great care so as to provide a congregational response to what has been done in their name by their minister, the whole concern collapses, and becomes merely a disorganized heap of pious actions, gone through in this order merely because the minister directs that this shall be done. It becomes at once an example of that sacerdotalism of which Geddes MacGregor so rightly complained in his recent book, *The Coming Reformation.*

In such a case, what is demanded in the chooser of the hymns is the kind of pastoral sensitiveness which will enable him to judge what hymn will best express, at that moment, in that service, what the congregation was waiting to say. To this must be added an intimate knowledge of the hymnal, so that the hymn which is right for the moment may be at once found and used. Then one sees the force of what Bernard Manning once wrote—writing as a Congregationalist churchman—that "hymns are our liturgy."

The fullness of this use of hymns as liturgy will be found where the rest of the service is of the most austere and simple kind. It was out of that situation, after all, that hymn singing first came to Englishmen through the work of Isaac Watts. The infinite charismatic variety of such worship is dear to the heirs of John Calvin, and in practice it is equally dear to those English Methodists whose heritage of hymnody is so incomparable: but Methodism of the English kind has again its own special emphasis which lies halfway between the Anglican emphasis on hymns as illustrating the church's teaching and the Congregational-Baptist emphasis on hymns as providing a congregational response to the movement of the liturgy.

The next point to notice, however, is this: that this kind of worship finds its natural home in a certain kind of society. Its historic home was in the Puritan meetinghouses of England (and of New England), where any kind of sumptuousness, in worship as in life, was frowned upon. Moreover, these meetinghouses were houses of family prayer rather than of public worship. Until the evangelical revival had transformed their outlook, they were neither large in size nor ostentatious in habit.

Two things have happened since then, one of which is conspicuous in Britain, the other of which is familiar in America. In Britain the Reformed churches have passed through a period of great prosperity

119

which brought a sense of status and, not infrequently, an ostentation that went beyond the boundary of vulgarity. Now they have very largely been obliged to retrench drastically, and, often in buildings far too large and portentous, they have lost the choirs which were once so valuable a status symbol, the anthems lie collecting dust on the vestry shelves, and the simple form of worship is forced back on them. New churches are built, small, modest, of a reasonable size for the expected congregation, and with small but often effective organs. The pomp of yesterday is as dead as Nineveh and Tyre. Out of its wreckage has come, in some places, a form of worship which in its freshness and modesty not only comes far nearer the Calvinist ideal but actually serves the modern Christian more effectively than the older kind did. In such a case, the hymn comes into its own again. But with a difference. When Puritan meetinghouses were meetinghouses, hymns were few, and often only by one or two authors, sung unaccompanied to a repertory of half a dozen tunes, or at best a dozen. The opulence of modern culture has given us not only hymnals of enormous range but congregations far better at learning new music and appreciating different forms of music than their ancestors of the eighteenth century were. There is, actually, no more exciting liturgical experience than to minister today to a reasonably sensitive and responsive congregation in conditions where plain economics preclude any kind of pomp, and where the adipose tissue has therefore fallen away from the service, showing once again how fine its bones are.

It is hardly so in the eastern part of America. There Reformed churches are very often buildings of great beauty, haunted by large congregations, staffed by more than one choir, adorned with massive organs and excellently trained musicians, and exercising a public ministry of considerable influence. And here we see at once a certain natural principle coming into operation. Whether or not you care for a prescribed liturgy, public behavior demands a certain decorum. Decorum is what at once supervenes in the prosperous and public-minded church. It expresses itself in ceremonial which may be very unlike traditional Romish ceremonials, but is observed with no less reverence by its devotees.

Obviously this has its dangers, but it is not my business to offer criticism of it. I note it only as a historic phenomenon. But its effect on the whole ethos of worship is profound. For once the presence of a very large congregation is presumed, and once the resources for developing church music (and for building imposing churches) are at hand, the service loses a good deal of that intimacy which the foregoing pattern of hymn choosing presupposes. Indeed, the service begins largely to overlap the liturgical traditions: for although it does not employ traditional liturgies and certainly does not use the same liturgical material from week to week, this kind of service is nonetheless highly ceremonious.

The following example comes from Riverside Church, New York. I am happy to quote in full (with permission) from the service paper because I can testify, having been present at the service, to its being a very finished example of Reformed worship in the society that Riverside serves.

The service (on July 29, 1962) ran as follows:

> Carillon Prelude
> Organ Prelude
> PROCESSIONAL HYMN, "Love divine" (P. 228)
> Call to Worship
> Introit [sung]
> Invocation and the Lord's Prayer
> HYMN, "From all that dwell below the skies" (P. 11)
> Reading from Scripture [Epistle]
> Anthem
> Pastoral Prayer [Choral Response]
> Offering, with Anthem.
> Choral Response
> HYMN, "Rise up, O men of God!" (P. 300)
> Sermon
> Prayer
> RECESSIONAL HYMN, "O Master Workman" (P. 412)
> Benediction
> Postlude

Now if this be compared with the Scottish order quoted a few pages back, it will be seen that where the Scottish order contained five hymns, each of which was in a position to carry liturgical significance, the Riverside service contains only two which carry such significance. The processional and recessional cover the entrance and the exit of the choir: their purpose is ceremonial rather than liturgical. And what is more, their choice really followed a principle different from that which would have obtained in the Scottish context, and different from that which governed the choice of the middle two in the Riverside service. What is more again, they were chosen on exactly the same principle on which a processional and recessional would be chosen at a Lutheran or Anglican Eucharist.

For observe: the processional hymn in this or an Anglican or Lutheran full service would be a hymn strictly of invocation: "Love divine" was so treated here. That is a legitimate way to treat it. And the recessional is quite properly, both in those other contexts and in this, a carol-like hymn that sends people out into the world with an inspiriting Christian song on their lips. In other words, these two hymns were chosen because of a certain general quality in their words and tunes, but not for the actual words they used. Now in the pure Reformed tradition this does not happen. What does happen we will show in a moment, but first observe the difference in the principle on which the other two hymns seem to have been chosen. "From all that dwell" corresponds to the first hymn in a simple Reformed service: it is specifically a hymn of praise in which the congregation declares its love of the God before whom it has now come. And "Rise up, O men of God" may well have been chosen with a view to the subject of the sermon immediately following, which happened to be "The Anatomy of a Rebel." These hymns were placed where they were after consideration had been given to their actual words, not to their general type.

With this compare the following selection in the Scottish context.

A Specimen Service from Scotland

The actual occasion was the morning of the second Sunday in Advent, 1962. The text of the sermon was Ps. 85:8: "I will hear what God the Lord will speak: for he will speak peace unto his people, and to his saints: but let them not turn again to folly." The second Sunday in Advent is, in Britain, widely kept as the day on which the revelation of himself by God through the Scriptures is the special subject of attention. The purpose of the sermon was to assist those who read the Scriptures to "hear what God the Lord will speak," even in times of doubt or other obstruction of the free course of the Word. This then is how the praise was chosen:

> PRAISE: "Wake, awake, for night is flying" (H. 3, P. 108, sts. 1-2; see 36-37)
> Prayers of Invocation and Confession
> Assurance of Pardon
> Address to Children (Ps. 27:1)
> PRAISE: "Mine eyes have seen the glory" (P. 443)
> Prayer with Children
> The Lord's Prayer
> Dismissal of Children
> Collection
> Intimations
> Prayer of Dedication
> PRAISE: "Lamp of our feet" (H. 400, P. 256)
> Readings from Psalm 85; I Timothy 3; John 5
> PRAISE: "The Lord will come and not be slow" (H. 312, P. 95)
> Sermon
> Prayers of Intercession and Thanksgiving
> PRAISE: "When we in darkness walk" (CH. 561, sts. 4-7)
> Blessing

These were the reasons for the choosing of these hymns.

1. "Wachet auf." This is a classic Advent hymn which marks the season unforgettably. It is unusual to place the most demanding hymn first in the service, but this hymn has recently been learned by the congregation and it is now safe to use it on such an occasion. Its mood of expectancy makes it particularly suitable for the opening of the service.

2. "Mine eyes have seen." Here is a hymn which is a good example of the principle mentioned in chapter 4, that for young people a touch of the picturesque can excuse a certain dogmatic lightness of weight. The Church Hymnary's selection of verses excludes the "circling camps" but includes "He is coming like the glory of the morning," which reflects "The Lord is my light and my salvation," the subject of the children's address.

3. "Lamp of our feet." Here we recall the special subject of the

123

day, and move nearer the subject upon which the lessons will be read.

4. "The Lord will come." Advent again, but this time in the context of the Psalter—the hymn is a cento from Milton's versification of three psalms, including that from which the text of the day came. The hymn also suggests a social concern in "Rise, God, judge thou the earth in might."

5. "When we in darkness walk." Here a very fine hymn was made out of an awkward one by omitting its first three verses (see Appendix B, p. 189). It was chosen especially for the verse which ran:

> Wait till the shadows flee;
> Wait thy appointed hour;
> Wait till the Bridegroom of thy soul
> Reveals His love with power.

This seemed to be the point toward which the sermon and the following prayers had led the congregation.[4]

It will be seen that the words of these hymns were chosen with considerable care. But perhaps it will also be seen that there is a touch of program building about the selection, in that meters, weights, and textures are circumspectly balanced. The service begins with what to British singers is a demanding and even exhausting hymn, although it is so magnificent. It is followed by a lyrical and untheological song, chosen for a special point, that goes to a rousing tune which children very much enjoy. The third and fourth hymns are in common meter and were sung to very simple psalm tunes, one of four lines, the other of eight. The last hymn is a rousing song by any standards, but the spiritual content of its words is more penetratingly and economically expressed than that of any of the others. Of the five hymns, four were easy to sing, two went to really popular and cheerful tunes, two went to psalm tunes which in Scotland are almost traditional. Two were in peculiar meters, three were in normal meters. The tunes, as it happened, were written

_____

[4] It may here be observed that there are a few examples—this is the most conspicuous one that I know—of hymns whose initial images (see page 110) are so unpromising as to be almost repulsive, but which can be rescued by leaving out the initial verse or verses. The opening lines of this hymn, by Augustus Toplady, are "Your harps, ye trembling saints, Down from the willows take."

respectively in 1596, 1915, 1615, 1709, and 1850.[5] We do not undertake always to achieve such symmetry as that. As to the words, they came from sixteenth-century Germany, nineteenth-century America, nineteenth-century England, seventeenth-century England, and eighteenth-century England—again a symmetry which was not deliberately sought.

But the aesthetic effect of hymns all of which come from the same period, affect the same style, use the same meter, or go to the same kind of tune, is undoubtedly deadening and should be avoided.

This means that the choice of hymns is, in such a situation, part of the preaching of the gospel. They surround the worshiper with the church's teaching, converging on the particular point which is being emphasized on that particular occasion.

This, as I say, cannot be achieved to anything like the same extent where the worship is more ceremonious and formal, and where a large choir performs one or two anthems (which, with the best will in the world, it is difficult to choose for their words). The effects in these more ceremonious places must be altogether broader, and the hymns cannot be expected to bear anything like so great a weight of teaching.

If then we have these two traditions running in parallel, the ceremonious and the Reformed, what advice ought we to offer to those who choose hymns in either of them? In the Reformed tradition the minister can give the matter all the skill, perceptiveness, and pastoral imagination he has. He ought to listen both to his congregation singing and to the opinions of his organist concerning tunes; but he will find the whole task far more rewarding if he knows his hymnbook and uses it as a precision instrument than if he chooses his praises at the last minute in the vestry.

But it would be quite wrong to say that where a service is much adorned with anthems, and hymns play a much smaller part, the task of careful choice can be neglected by the chooser of the praise. If certain hymns must be chosen because they are of a kind suitable for procession or recession, let them nonetheless be good literature and good music, seasonable and illuminating. There is no case for

[5] I must ask the reader to take my word for the fact that I noticed this deployment of the tunes over the centuries only when I was in the course of writing this chapter, and that it was not for this reason that I chose to use this service as an example!

saying that "anything will do to get the choir in and out." Great profundity is probably out of place: and certainly a choir in procession cannot be expected to lead the singing with much effect, so the tune must be a "good runner." But beyond this, fine words of an invocatory kind are not far to seek: nor are inspiriting words for the closing recessional. Elsewhere in the service all the care that goes into the choice of hymns in an all-Reformed service is necessary and rewarding.

Where there is none of the Reformed hymn culture, where hymns are primarily creedal or primarily illustrations of church teaching, they still ought to be read with critical care before they are chosen; and where their imagery is misleading or fails to communicate with the contemporary congregation, they may well be avoided.

Special Occasions

There are occasions when all of us have to bow to traditional custom, when our hymns, or some of them, are dictated by social and even secular custom rather than by any theological impulse. One of these occasions is the Harvest Festival in Britain, or the Thanksgiving Day service in the United States, at both of which certain hymns seem to be perennial. One of these provides a good example of the principle that there is no need to be negligent just because custom rather than liturgy dictates the choice of hymns.

· Consider the hymn "Come, ye thankful people, come" (H. 137, P. 461). There seems to be hardly any point at which this hymn is not open to criticism. But custom forbids us to criticize it. Nonetheless we will do so here.

In the first place, nearly everybody thinks of it as a hymn of thanksgiving. That is because its initial image is one of thanks for the harvest. But in fact only its first verse is thanksgiving for the harvest. The rest is a homily on certain biblical texts in which "harvest" appears, and which converge on the theme of the last judgment. It is extremely doubtful whether this later imagery makes any impact on congregations at all; this is the less probable now that the hymn is firmly wedded to a tune which sounds so jaunty and cheerful about it all. The tune was written originally for a missionary hymn on Christ's triumph by James Montgomery: "Hark, the song of Jubilee."

In the second place, at two points the words say what singers often cannot mean. It may not often happen in America: but in Britain one constantly hears a congregation sing "All is safely gathered in" on the third Sunday in September, which is bound to be nonsense, and in a year of bad weather, heartless nonsense. And who really means what he appears to mean when he sings:

> Give his angels charge at last
> In the fire the tares to cast,
> But the fruitful ears to store
> In his garner evermore (st. 3, ll. 4-8).

The tune makes a fortissimo yell at "But the fruitful" inevitable. But can one sing so blithely about the fearsome implications of the last judgment? Ought one to attempt to do so on a cheerful creature-ly festival like Harvest or Thanksgiving? Is this not really an incongruity that comes precious near to hypocrisy? How good it would be if these lines, all thirty-two of them, were banished from such celebrations. I can recall that an eminent English clergyman of that Anglican church out of which this hymn originally came, who is now precentor of the Cathedral at Coventry, described these lines in a broadcast in 1950 as "vile." The word may be too strong for some. I am content with "substandard." It may be observed that the editors of the *Pilgrim Hymnal* clearly thought their value traditional rather than real, and placed alongside them a hymn using its first verse and sixteen other lines by Anna L. Barbauld and others. It is not a very successful piece of literature, but at least it does keep to the subject (see P. 462).

It is certainly high time that the church ceased to be "conformed to the world" at such points as this. National occasions so often produce second-rate hymnody. In times past when there was little to choose from, those who used it were less blameworthy. But if on a day of national thanksgiving men want to sing thanksgiving, let them sing "Now thank we all our God" (as, to be sure, they do); and if they want to sing of judgment, let them sing "Lord Christ, when first thou cam'st to men" (H. 522, P. 325), which at least does face the singer with its august subject from its opening line.

Hymns should never be sung because they are customary. They

should only be sung because they express Christian teaching, and promote Christian teaching, in a manner which will communicate itself to the congregation for whom they are chosen. To this rule there are no exceptions. Successful communication is made only by good literature and good music. Any falling away from this standard is "conformity with the world," and no prosperity or status ought ever to become an excuse for such conformity.

7. On
Editing Hymnals

The Prevailing Fashion and Its History

In the last chapter we noted that the first factor limiting the choice of hymns in any community is the selection of hymns in the hymnal there used. Here we will elaborate that point; for the task of editors is a highly responsible one, and the effect it will have on the morale of those for whom they do their work is likely to be profound.

Hymnals of the modern kind are now edited according to a fashion something over a hundred years old. This is the fashion of placing a tune alongside a hymn and regarding this as the right tune for that hymn. Not everybody realizes how comparatively recently this practice began. In former days it was customary for hymns and tunes to be published in separate volumes, and for a tune book to be only in the hands of the precentor or the organist. Two of the most famous nineteenth-century tune books were *The Psalmist,* edited by Vincent Novello in four volumes of one hundred tunes each between 1836 and 1843, and *The Bristol Tune Book* (first edition, 1863: third and last edition, containing over nine hundred tunes, 1881). Among the British denominations, the Congregationalists produced their first book of hymns set to tunes in 1887, *The Congregational Church Hymnal* (this is, however, not to take account of a private venture, *The Congregational Psalmist,* printed a few years before); the Baptists in 1900, the *Baptist Church Hymnal;* the Methodists in 1877, *Wesley's Hymns, with tunes;* and the Presbyterian Church of England in 1885 *Church Praise*. The Church of Scotland's first music edition was *The Church Hymnary* of 1898. All these bodies up to then used books of words with separate books of tunes.

As for the Church of England, it has never had an "official" hymnary as the dissenting denominations have had, or as the Episcopal Church of the United States has. But as a matter of fact it was the publication in 1861 of the phenomenally successful *Hymns Ancient and Modern* which attracted attention to this custom of setting each hymn to its proper tune. *Hymns Ancient and Modern* was the last of a series of private ventures in hymnbook publishing which had taken place in the 1850's, and which had sought to apply this method. Of these the most interesting are William Mercer's *Church Psalter and Hymn Book* (1854), which at each page opening provided three, four, or even six hymns in not more than two meters and not more than two tunes to go with them; Richard Chope's *Congregational Hymn and Tune Book* (1857), an early venture in the "one hymn, one tune" style, sensitively edited and later enlarged (1862); and Thomas Helmore's *The Hymnal Noted* (1852), an early essay in plainsong notation and the revival of medieval music. But *Hymns Ancient and Modern* in its first music edition of 1861 combined wide success with the careful application of this new principle. And as a consequence collocations of hymn and tune which are now regarded on both sides of the Atlantic as indivorcible were first introduced to the hymn singing world. There are many examples of hymns and tunes both older than 1861 and published before that date whose association we owe to this book; among these are "O God, our help in ages past" sung to "St. Anne," "The Head that once was crown'd with thorns" to "St. Magnus," "How sweet the Name of Jesus sounds" to "St. Peter," and "There is a green hill far away" to "Horsley." This is to take no account of the new music introduced in that book which at once commended itself as the inevitable setting for its hymn, like John B. Dykes' tune "Nicaea," for "Holy, Holy, Holy" and W. H. Monk's "Eventide" for "Abide with me," both of which hymns had received earlier settings.

Nowadays it is very unusual for a hymnbook to be published in separate volumes for tunes and words. Perhaps the last notable one to be so published was *The Christian Hymnary* (Churches of Christ,

1938). We now assume that each hymn will have its tune, and that tunes will not often be repeated for different hymns.

The historical reason for this change of custom was the heightened sense of music aroused in the people of both countries by the extraordinary increase of interest during the second quarter of the nineteenth century in choral music. John P. Hullah and Joseph Mainzer in Britain, and Lowell Mason in the United States, gave great impetus to movements that encouraged ordinary people to sing, and showed them how enjoyable choral song could be. This created a demand for, and a capacity to render, a wider repertory of hymn tunes and an impatience with the very narrow repertory with which all but the English Methodists were familiar at the beginning of the century. Indeed, the effects of this choral revival went much further than this: for it became the custom, particularly in the successful dissenting churches of England, for the whole congregation to add anthems to its hymn repertory, and up to a generation ago it was still customary in these circles to publish a large selection of simple anthems bound in with the hymns and psalms. The anthems in the dissenting hymnals were designed originally for congregational singing. Only later did they pass into the keeping of the choir, and the reason for this was a new movement of musical appreciation which supervened on that of musical amateur performance. The hymn singing habit in both countries has now undergone a further change. Whereas in the days of the first music editions of hymnals, hymns were thought of as choral pieces for everybody to sing (and the style of such as Dykes and Stainer was encouraged), they are now regarded as a very distinct kind of church music, primarily for unison singing and sharply distinguished from the choral music that is the choir's business.

Now we have already referred to the two distinct customs of printing music editions which prevail in America and in Britain. In Britain the words are interlined only when there is doubt, because of an irregular meter, about the manner of fitting them to the music. In America it appears to be the almost universal custom to interline all hymns, at any rate for the first few stanzas. Our comment on the wisdom of this procedure has already been made. But there is this now to add: that whereas the custom in Britain is to provide the choir with music copies and the congregation with words-only

131

copies of the hymnal, in the United States it is not at all uncommon to find every singer provided with a full music edition. And in this the United States is far ahead of Britain on the road of wisdom. It remains a scandal that in Britain music copies of hymnals remain so scarce, and hardly any publisher has deemed it worth his while to risk publishing a melody edition, with one line of music, for congregational use. No publisher of a hymnal in the Lutheran Church of Germany would dream of putting out a hymnal for congregational use without giving the melody with the words: and it is now true that words-only editions in the United States are hard to find. The British publisher will say that his smaller constituency and the conservatism of his constituents makes the offering of melody editions prohibitively expensive; but economics do not tell the whole story.

We are here concerned with the effect, and not the morality, of the wide dissemination of music editions. This ought to be that no hymn proves to be impracticable. If everyone has the score before him, there are, it is supposed, few who cannot train themselves to follow the indications of the printed notes. American editors work on this principle. British editors work on the principle that if the tune set to the hymn is not known, and the meter is not a peculiar one, then the tune can easily be changed. This is easier to do when the words are not interlined; but unless a choir is singing from stalls on which it can lay its hymnals at singing height (and can therefore comfortably use two books, one open at the words and the other at the alternative tune), the discomfort this causes always produces complaints from the singers, which are wholly justifiable. In America it is assumed that tunes will not be changed.

But if the congregation still insists on singing by ear, even when it has the music before it, then the repertory of hymns in that church will be restricted to hymns whose given tunes are familiar; and those which go to tunes that the congregation will not learn will not be sung at all. Editors have to remember all the time that they live in an imperfect society.

But our main question here is this: if the chooser of the hymns wants to follow the kind of methods we have here been advocating, what does he ask of his editors? The question would be put slightly differently in Britain from the way it would be put in the United

States, but basically it is the same question—"Will you please give me a book that is easy to use intelligently?"

Examples of This Fashion

Hymnals are now edited almost according to a stereotyped form. Very little attention appears to have been paid to the arrangement of the hymns within a book for at least a generation. The first suggestion we would here make to any who are editing a new hymnal is that they consider how far their normal table of contents is relevant to the necessities of public worship. Consider some typical tables from hymnals on both sides of the Atlantic (numbers in parentheses show total hymns in each section):

The Hymnal 1940 (Episcopal)

The Christian Year	(111)
Saints' Days and Holy Days	(25)
Thanksgiving and National Days	(12)
Morning and Evening	(36)
Sacraments and Other Rites	(44)
Litanies	(6)
Hymns for Children	(18)
Missions	(13)
General Hymns	(335)
	(total: 600)

The English Hymnal (Church of England)

The Christian Year	(173)
Saints' Days and Other Holy Days	(80)
Times and Seasons	(46)
Sacraments and Other Rites	(61)
General Hymns	(169)
Special Occasions	(24)
Church and People	(23)
Mission Services	(19)
At Catechism	(27)
Processional Hymns	(34)
Litanies	(10)
	(total: 656)

133

The Church Hymnary (Presbyterian)

GOD: HIS BEING, WORKS, AND WORD

The Holy Trinity (7)
God in Creation, Providence,
 and Redemption (32)
The Lord Jesus Christ: His In-
 carnation, Life, Death,
 Resurrection, Ascension,
 Intercession, Second Coming
 and Glory (141)
The Holy Spirit and the
 Scriptures (15)

THE CHURCH

The Communion of Saints (23)
Worship (including morning &
 evening hymns) (76)
Sacraments and Rites (29)
Service (31)
Missions (26)

THE CHRISTIAN LIFE

The Gospel Call (9)
Penitence and Faith (17)
Love and Gratitude (22)
Peace and Joy (11)
Prayer, Aspiration, and Holiness (35)
Brotherly Love (10)
Consecration and Discipleship (29)
Conflict and Victory (16)
Trust and Resignation (23)
Pilgrimage and Rest (23)
Death, Resurrection, and the Life
 Everlasting (16)

TIMES AND SEASONS (23)
TRAVELLERS AND THE ABSENT (7)
NATIONAL HYMNS (17)
HOME AND SCHOOL (31)
MISSION SERVICES (29)
DOXOLOGIES (6)

(total: 713)

Pilgrim Hymnal (Congregational)

WORSHIP

Adoration and Praise	(31)
Morning	(12)
Evening	(16)
Close of Worship	(4)

GOD THE FATHER

Works in Creation: Providence: Grace	(39)

OUR LORD JESUS CHRIST

Advent to Ascension: Presence and Guidance: Character and Glory	(128)

THE HOLY SPIRIT	(15)
THE TRINITY	(6)
THE BIBLE	(8)

THE CHURCH OF CHRIST

Nature, Unity, Fellowship	(17)
Sacraments (two)	(16)
Mission in the World	(13)
Communion of Saints	(7)

THE CHRISTIAN LIFE

Gospel Call and Response	(19)
Prayer	(5)
Hope, Joy, Peace	(9)
Faith and Aspiration	(16)
Pilgrimage and Conflict	(28)
Consecration	(19)

THE KINGDOM OF GOD ON EARTH

Brotherhood and Service	(15)
Justice	(5)
The Nation	(15)
World Peace	(9)

SEASONS	(12)

SPECIAL SERVICES AND OCCASIONS

Marriage and the Family: Funerals: Ordinations: Church Dedications	(13)
CHILDREN AND YOUTH	(18)
THE NATIONAL ANTHEM	(1)

(total: 496)

Methodist Hymnal (In preparation; revision authorized in 1964)

I. THE GOSPEL AND
   CHRISTIAN EXPERIENCE

  A. *Praise of God*
    1. Adoration
    2. Majesty and Power
    3. Creation
    4. Providence
    5. Love and Mercy

  B. *The Gospel of Jesus Christ*
    1. His Name and Glory
    2. His Mercy and Grace
    3. Call
    4. Repentance—Forgiveness
    5. Atonement and Salvation

  C. *The Holy Spirit*

  D. *The Christian Life*
    1. Faith and Regeneration
    2. Discipleship and Witness
    3. Consecration and Stewardship
    4. Brotherhood and Service
    5. Trust and Assurance
    6. Hope, Joy and Peace
    7. Courage in Conflict
    8. Prayer and Aspiration
    9. Christian Perfection
    10. Death and Eternal Life

II. THE CHURCH

  A. *Nature and Mission*
  B. *Unity—Fellowship*
  C. *Baptism*
  D. *The Lord's Supper*
  E. *Marriage*

  F. *The Ministry*
  G. *Dedications*

III. THE CHRISTIAN YEAR

  A. *Advent Season*
  B. *Christmastide*
  C. *Epiphany Season*
  D. *Lenten Season*
    1. Passion
    2. Palm Sunday
    3. Holy Week
  E. *Eastertide*
    1. Easter
    2. Ascension and Enthronement
  F. *Pentecost Season*
  G. *Kingdomtide*

IV. TIMES, SEASONS, OCCASIONS

  A. *The Lord's Day*
  B. *Morning—Evening*
  C. *Seasonal Hymns*
    1. The Changing Year—Covenant
    2. Rural Life (Rogation)
    3. The Christian Home
    4. Harvest and Thanksgiving
  D. *Schools and College*
  E. *Anniversaries*
    1. Aldersgate
    2. Reformation and All Saints
  F. *Travel*
  G. *The City, the Nation, and the World*

Criticism of This Fashion: With Support from John Wesley

That is quite enough. If we enumerated the tables of any twenty current hymnals on either side of the ocean, they would show (with one or two exceptions which we are about to notice) no significant variation on this pattern. It is serviceable, no doubt, and we are all used to it. The one difference between Episcopal custom and non-Episcopal is the different emphasis placed on the Church Year, which is so called in Episcopal books, but which is theologically categorized in the others. "Christmas" for Episcopals becomes "His Incarnation" for the Dissenters. But that is nowadays a trifling distinction. Hardly more significant is it that normally Episcopal books begin with the Church Year while non-Episcopal ones begin with the glory of God. It is easy to see the difference of habit which this implies: but none of this is of more than slight significance beside the dreary repetitiveness of all these tables of contents.

It might be noted against the Episcopals that for a hundred years now—yes, ever since that fateful *Hymns Ancient and Modern*—they have permitted themselves the disastrous heading of "General Hymns." G. W. Briggs, a distinguished clergyman of the Church of England, whose hymns are well known in Britain and in the United States, used constantly to protest against this, and ask with contempt, "What is a general hymn?" This question we reiterate.

The idea of a "general hymn" is itself a dissuasive from the sensible use of hymns. But on the other hand, the persistent association of hymns with certain seasons or certain concepts often promotes habits that drain the hymns of much of their vitality.

One hymnal recently published in England has entirely forsworn the use of section headings. This is the *English Hymnal Service Book* (1962), a book derived from *The English Hymnal* of 1906 and 1933, but to a large extent modifying the policy of the original book. This contains one series of 298 hymns in the alphabetical order of their first initial letter. This series is followed by two short appendices bringing the total to 336. But in the main body of the book each hymn is given a heading which indicates its specific use. "Come, Holy Ghost," for example, is marked "Whitsuntide, Ordination, Confirmation." The ubiquitous "General" is allowed to appear over some hymns; but often with second directions alongside it. And a very comprehensive subject index, with no fewer than 139 cue words, guides the chooser to hymns appropriate to his subject or occasion. "Holy Communion" thus gets two whole columns of hymns, and other occasions are far better served than they are by the conventional sectionalizations.

The Methodist Hymnal, at present in preparation, and expected in a few years' time, shows in its editors a consciousness that the table of contents ought to be taken seriously. In the editorial report published privately after the first stage of the revision, the desire of the committee was expressly stated to be "to formulate a system of classifying hymns according to the traditional topical approach, and the growing emphasis on the Christian Year." The resulting table (see above p. 136) presents an appearance of originality. This hymnal will be the first to present the system of the Christian Year at quite a late stage in the body of the book. It will be unusual to find the Christmas hymns among the third or fourth hundred. *The Methodist Hymn Book* in England uses a much more conventional arrangement.

Not all Christian singers would feel comfortable with the Methodist arrangement as it will be in the new United States book; but the reason for its adoption is perfectly clear and rational, within the special terms of reference of Methodism. I am allowed to quote from a private communication here, which expresses some of the chief aims of the committee:

Among other things, the new hymnal will (a) recover a good many eighteenth-century texts, particularly Watts and Wesley; (b) provide for the first time in any American Methodist Hymnal an expression of the full Christian Year; and (c) in the musical realm, increase the amount of chorale, plainsong, Psalter, and folk hymnody.

In other words, the aim is to treat historic *Methodism* more seriously, and to bring out more prominently its special aims. Methodism historically laid emphasis precisely on these three things—eighteenth-century texts (obviously, it was an eighteenth-century movement), the Christian Year (because it was the creation of two

Anglican priests who knew and loved the *Book of Common Prayer*), and a great variety of music, especially the folk music of the eighteenth-century Englishman (which was, broadly speaking, not what we now call folk song but light opera).

This is not to say (as we shall see in a moment) that the Wesleys arranged their hymnbooks as this one is arranged. But it is to say that the new editors are specially concerned to produce a modern interpretation of authentic Methodism. And this one sees primarily in the heading of their first main section—"The Gospel and Christian Experience." There, anyhow, is an authentic Wesleyan word —experience! No other hymnal places *that* in the position of primary honor. The new emphasis contrasts very strongly with that of the 1935 American Methodist hymnal, whose table of contents provides not four but twelve main sections, with as curious a cross classification as any that one could find in such a place:

Worship
God
Jesus Christ
The Holy Spirit
The Gospel
The Christian Life
The Living Church
The Christian Home and Family
Hymns for Children
The Kingdom of God
The Eternal Life
Special Seasons and Services   (Total: 564).

It has always been a matter of controversy within Methodism, and between Methodists and other believers, whether Methodism is or is not a "Dissent." Historically, Methodism was not a Dissenting church in England, but was regarded by the Wesleys (however much the Anglicans disagreed with them) as an order within the English Church. It was only in the nineteenth century that Methodism developed the ethos of Dissent; this was due to the influence of the post-Wesley Primitive movement in Methodism.

But the plain fact is that since 1904 in England the Methodist hymnals have presented an outward appearance which has everything in common with Dissenting hymnals (Baptist, Congregationalist, Presbyterian), and almost nothing in common with Anglican hymnals. That was the case also with the 1935 American book. The new book seeks to correct this, not by presenting an "Episcopal" appearance, with the emphasis weighted towards the church and its rites and away from Christian experience, but a book which presents Methodist "experience" in close alliance with a liturgical sense which the Wesleys themselves were never without. This new hymnal, then, is not primarily a "Dissenting" hymnal, but much more strictly an evangelical hymnal. It is, as it were, not now thought so necessary to emphasize the differences between Methodist and any Episcopal "establishment" as to emphasize what Methodism *adds* to the total store of Christian church experience.

But I am now going to venture the point that even this entirely praiseworthy reconsideration of the table of contents leaves a certain number of aspirations unsatisfied. First, let us look at history. In the classics of early hymnody you have three quite different approaches to the use of hymns. Isaac Watts's *Hymns and Spiritual Songs* (1707) is arranged in no discernible order, except that the small collection in Book III is composed of Communion hymns, and occasionally hymns on kindred subjects appear in a group. Philip Doddridge's *Hymns,* first published complete after his death in the edition of Job Orton (1755), are arranged according to the biblical order of the texts they expound. And the first hymnbook of the Wesleys, published in 1779, has the following table of contents:

PART I

Containing Introductory Hymns

Sect.   I. Exhorting Sinners
          II. Describing 1. The Pleasantness of Religion
          ....2. The Goodness of God.
          ....3. Death
          ....4. Judgment
          ....5. Heaven
          ....6. Hell
          III. Praying for a Blessing

Strange words perhaps, but how candidly that table of contents shows what the genius of the book, and of the society that used it, was meant to be. The community for which Doddridge wrote his hymns was a community of Bible readers, and their worship was from end to end biblical. The community of which Wesley was the leader was a gathering of men of ripe Christian experience pledged to share their experience with others. For Wesley, every hymn had its place in the scheme, and the scheme was none other than the scheme of Christian salvation.

By the same token, what do our tables of contents convey concerning the ethos of the communities which use them? Certainly the situation for us is vastly different: we have hymns by hundreds of authors living all through the Christian era to arrange in our hymn-nals; Watts and Doddridge had only their own, and Wesley's table of authors, had he provided one, would have filled only a few lines.

But nonetheless there is something unsatisfactory and ambiguous about our hymn arrangements. And the real reason for this is, I suspect, that in all modern hymnals there is what the ancient logi-cians called "cross classification." If we compare any of the modern tables exemplified with Wesley's, we see what this means. Wesley had a single scheme and pursued it throughout—and all his head-ings follow it. Part I—introductory (that is, of the introduction to religion, not of the introduction to a service); Part II—religion; Part III—for mourners (that is, penitents or seekers); Part IV—for believers; Part V—for the society.

Wesley's Table shows that his society is indeed a society. Our tables show that the church is an institution. And if we use that word in a pejorative sense we mean to convey that the church, as it shows itself in its editorial work, is more concerned with an ap-pearance of order than with the proclamation of a consistent pur-pose. What else can we feel when in one book "Travelers and the Absent" is a heading coordinate with "God: His Being, Works, and Word"? What kind of misleading speech is it that places "Missions" outside a section headed "General Hymns," and makes it coordinate with "Saints Days and Holy Days"? (The answer here is: the kind of speech that relegates overseas missionary work, like the Feast of St. Matthew, to one Sunday in the year.) Another table makes "Mis-sions" coordinate with "The Sacraments" and "The Burial of the Dead." Yet another, somewhat hilariously, makes "Mission Services" coordinate with "General Hymns." This is *The English Hymnal,* and in its 1933 edition it adds a headline in very small italic over the first hymn in the "Mission Services" section explaining that the hymns that follow are not suitable for general use. They are, of course, what others know as "Gospel Hymns," but they include "O Jesus, I have promised" and "Rest of the weary."

Consequences of This Fashion

This is the appearance of order covering confusion. And we have already mentioned some of the reasons why we believe this to be a defect with important consequences, and not merely an offense to the pedantic. Few habits do more harm to modern missionary work than the relegation of a number of hymns to a section called "Missions." Two consequences are irresistible; that those hymns will be sung on missionary occasions alone, and that on such occasions the chooser of hymns will take his praise wholly or mainly from that section: thus the missionary occasion becomes stereotyped, habitual, and tainted with unreality and irrelevance. Marriages similarly are often reduced to ignorant formality by the assumption that only hymns in the "Marriage" section of the book should be used when they are celebrated. Editors find increasing difficulty in deciding what are children's hymns. And the segregation of certain hymns of which the editors do not approve into a section labeled "Mission Services" looks uncomfortably like a hymnological application of the situation described in Jam. 2:3, "And say to the poor, stand thou there, or sit here under my footstool."

It would be most unwise even to appear to be prescribing a pattern for future hymnbooks; but it is not too much, perhaps, to suggest that a good deal of vitality would be added to the hymnals of the future if their editors began with the table of contents and considered new systems of compiling them. And their object in doing this might well be to increase the availability and relevance of the hymns included in their book, and perhaps release many hymns from the prison of association into which they have been thrust by custom.

For example, "Christ, whose glory fills the skies" (H. 153, P. 43) —is this really a morning hymn? Is it primarily a morning hymn? Answer: First, it is a hymn about conversion (in Wesley's 1779 hymnbook it is in the section "For the Society Praying"); second, it is not even unsuitable for singing in the afternoon or the evening. The time of day is really no part of the hymn's real content. In this it is utterly unlike, say, "Awake, my soul, and with the sun" (H. 151, P. 32). But then consider the hymn, "Awake, my soul": it is quite misleading to place it in a section generally labeled "Morning," because its application is to a *weekday* morning; it is wholly unsuitable to a service on Sunday, and especially to one beginning in the middle of the morning. Yet another morning hymn lays traps for the unwary—Wesley's famous "Forth in thy name" (H. 150, P.

406) . If this be called "morning," once again it is unsuitable for Sunday morning, unless it is quite clear that he who sings it will not be in church again until next Sunday. For churches which hold two services, one of which is in the evening, the proper place for it is at the end of the evening service. In certain hymnals it has been removed from the "Morning" section. The *Pilgrim Hymnal* is one, and *The Church Hymnary* and *The Methodist Hymn Book* in Britain do this also.

Or consider certain evening hymns. How much is added to their significance if the common factor of "evening" is suppressed and the other subjects they deal with are brought out. "At even, ere the sun was set" (P. 55) deals with Christ's ministry of healing; "All praise to thee, my God, this night" (H. 165, P. 57) with God's protection; "Sun of my soul" (H. 166, P. 50) is a prayer of intercession, and so is "Now the day is over" (H. 172, P. 51) . "O gladsome light" (H. 176, P. 49) is a doxology of praise to Christ; "The day thou gavest" (H. 179, P. 47) is a hymn of the worldwide church; "The duteous day" (H. 181, P. 53) is a hymn of God's creation and of the promise of heaven; "The sun is sinking fast" (H. 183) is a hymn of the passion—and so on. Indeed, it could fairly be said that any hymn designated an evening hymn which has not a primary theological subject is probably otiose, and a means of promoting sentimentality. The intelligent choice of evening hymns would remove a good deal of sentimentality from evening services. A guide to this is much needed from editors.

And then there is the difficult question concerning Advent hymns, whether they are primarily dealing with the first Advent or the second coming. "O come, O come, Emmanuel" (H. 2, P. 110) is as clearly a dramatic reliving of the historic moments of preparation for the nativity, as "Lo! he comes" (H. 5) is a dramatic preview of the last things. In the Advent season both kinds of thought inevitably come to the worshiper's mind, since he lives, as the theologians say, "between the times." But there is a difference between association and confusion, and one of the reasons why the Advent season has been overlaid by proleptic Christmas celebrations is no doubt the difficulty that Christians have had in forming a clear notion of what Advent means. The hymns have not helped, because they have added to the confusion.

An Experiment in a New Pattern

Is there any means by which editors of the future can help their people to use their hymnals as an illumination of their faith rather than as an instrument of obscurity? I shall now make one suggestion which I hope my readers will see to be only one of many that could be made, and that could better be made by others of other traditions.

I shall here make my suggestions from a Protestant standpoint: I am a Protestant, and I can do no other. Let us begin by asking what is the source of all Christian doctrine for Protestants. It is, of course, the Scriptures. Now I am aware that many Protestants (and I am myself of their number) would be dissatisfied with so simple and bald a statement. Doctrine is organic, and in its formation the church, and the inward testimony of the conscience, play a decisive part. The church was historically in being before what we now call the Bible was canonized. This can be agreed; but in this particular field we are dealing with a small part of the church's practice, and the important thing to notice about this field of hymnody is that it is a literary field. It is within the general field of the communication of Christian doctrine through words and images. So is the Bible. It is therefore, I think, legitimate (though I do not claim it is the only possible course) to begin with the Bible.

Let us next say that the Bible is a record of decisive human experience and that hymns are the expression of contemporary human experience. In the Scriptures we learn of God's ways with man; in hymns we respond to what we have heard of the Word of God.

Then let us say that just as the Bible is a book of books, which can be read either as a precious collection of sacred oracles or as a continuous record of God's dealings with men, so a hymnal which really expressed the church's faith ought to be usable either as a collection of sacred lyrics or as a book which can be read as a kind of commentary on the story the Bible tells.

Maybe we have gone too fast here. Is it necessary again to state our conviction that a hymnal ought to be *read* as well as sung from?

What kind of hymnal would we produce if its hymns were arranged in a manner that recalled the arrangement of the biblical books?

Well, at once we shall see that it will not begin where the usual hymnals begin—with Advent or with the Trinity. Where does the Old Testament begin? Why, with creation, with a dramatic picture (followed at once by a moralistic variant of the same picture) of God as Maker of all things visible and invisible. Let that, then, be our first section: hymns that express man's awareness of the majesty of God, an innocent and blissful awareness, with perhaps a touch of primitive awe and even terror. Not the whole story, only the beginning of the story. But it is where the Bible begins: God is and God made.

Then at once the Old Testament leads to the fall: to an expression of man's conviction that the created world is not as God designed it to be, and that he, man, is responsible for its sorrow.

After this comes a long section, comprising the rest of the books of the Law, which primarily stresses two things: God's new revelation of himself in the moral law, and life as a pilgrimage from exile toward home. These two themes are intertwined in the books of Exodus, Leviticus, Numbers, and Deuteronomy as we now have them.

Then come the historical books, which show how the will of God is done and how it is flouted, as men learn to live with one another; as they learn, painfully, how the new revelation is to be harmonized with the natural order of living in families and nations, how the word of God can be heard in politics and social affairs.

The prophets follow, with their various interpretations of the same message—that redemption and judgment and forgiveness are in the hands of God, that God still loves his world and looks for man's response, and that man may approach the awesome mystery whose beauty was in the ancient time supposed (Exodus 33) to be death to any who looked on it.

Then, only then, did Christ come. Then we learned of his incarnation, his ministry, his passion and death, his resurrection, and his ascension. Then the church was formed, and the life of the Holy Spirit was poured out on the church. Then could men of wisdom such as Paul and Peter speak of the new commandment. Then were the saints born, and then could men see (because they could dare to look) far ahead to the consummation of all things.

Now before we go into detail, let us mark one thing. There are passages in the Old Testament that are as rough and crude and dreadful as human life itself. (Of course there is no wild imagination: the worst things recorded in the Old Testament are no worse than any man who has lived through the twentieth century has heard of or seen.) On the other hand there are passages, like Isa. 52:13-53:12, which positively seem to touch the floor of the New Testament. You can hear the gospel coming when you read Psalm 85; you can hear the teaching of Christ often in Jeremiah. But especially is the Psalter full of Christ (as Christ's recorded words are full of it). We need not, in making our selection, be afraid of the inevitable Christian allusion in many hymns whose primary image is "Old Testament." We could indeed include a section corresponding to the Psalter of metrical Psalms, many of which are deliberately "Christianized" by such writers as Isaac Watts, Henry Lyte, and James Montgomery.

But the most remarkable thing about our hymnal would be the fact that it recognizes that many hymns are an exactly right expression of the condition of a Christian who is, at the moment, "in the Old Testament." We are not in the New Testament all the time, or even most of the time. Our vision is not "open." We fall away and come back and fall away again.

Any reader of this book will have noticed how often thoughtful Christians say, "I can't sing these hymns: they are for better men than I," or more simply, "I can't sing what I don't believe." The occasional ecstatic utterance of Charles Wesley, for example, often takes us much further than we are willing to go. True, a hymn like "And can it be" is the kind of hymn which by sheer force of its argument and imagery drags the singer, as it were, out of a state of sloth or despair into a state of hope. But this cannot be relied on. There is a place in a hymnal for hymns of high evangelical content, and there is equally a place for hymns primarily concerned with experience here and now. It is often the failure to distinguish between the terrific demands and assumptions of "Rock of ages" and the much more easygoing spiritual demand of "City of God"—and the failure to see the proper virtues of both—that leads to so much ineffective hymn choosing.

Old Testament Images

Now let us see how our hymnal sections might work out.[1]

Section I. Creation

A. GOD THE CREATOR

In this section, include such hymns on creation (without too deep spiritual undertones) as:

All creatures of our God and King (P. 64)
The duteous day (H. 181, P. 53)
The spacious firmament (H. 309, P. 72)

B. OUR KNOWLEDGE OF NATURE

A subsection offering hymns especially suitable for a scientific age could well follow. Of these there are few in American hymnals at present. "The duteous day" might perhaps be transferred here. Others might be

O Lord of hosts, all heaven possessing (EH. 458)
Lord, my weak thought in vain would climb (SP. 563)
Almighty Father of all things that be (CH. 503)

Note that this last has a reference to the redemption of nature through the cross. But its primary image is man's creative activity, so I suggest that it go here.

Section II. Sin and Forgiveness

Here at once is trouble. How exactly can we sing about sin? What even are we to call this section? If the Scriptures are our guide, the primary subject is the defacement of creation. But Christians cannot sing about that. Penitence in itself does not move us to song. We need some hymns here that fearlessly set out the human situation and that proclaim the gospel concerning it, which is forgiveness. We will not yet list hymns whose primary subject is redemption through Christ. They will come later. We want hymns of dark color, honestly recording man's rebellion and the mighty act that God made to recall him from it.

Before we go any further, notice two things which this discussion

[1] See Appendix A for a synopsis of the table here worked out.

has brought to our minds. If we begin editing a hymnal in this fashion, we may find that some old hymns we thought had passed into desuetude will come alive again, and that there are some gaps which require filling with new hymns. In respect of this last, our editor will begin to dictate letters to the best authors he knows and ask for these new hymns. But in respect of the first point, consider what might be done here by a revival of that great hymn, "Great God of wonders," by Samuel Davies of Princeton. Its language is here and there somewhat rough, but the version in *Congregational Praise* is still full of vital energy (see CP. 67). That would do for this section. So would:

Come, let us to the Lord our God (CP. 386)
My God, how wonderful thou art (H. 284)
Thou hidden love of God (H. 464)

Section III. Pilgrimage

In this section the hymns deal with God's revelation of himself through the moral law. Hymns on the Scriptures themselves are appropriate here, and hymns on simple moral themes such as:

Awake, my soul, and with the sun (H. 151, P. 32)
O God of truth, whose living Word (H. 547)
A charge to keep I have (MHB. 578)

Then hymns which express the idea of life as a pilgrimage whose leader and provider is the Lord would follow:

Guide me, O thou great Jehovah (H. 434, P. 93)
O God of Bethel (H. 497, P. 389)
Sometimes a light surprises (H. 443)

Section IV. Human Relations and Service

How are men, thus created and thus fallen, to see their natural human groups—often warring groups—sanctified by the revelation of God? Here is the place for hymns that usually appear in "National" sections, those that come under "Social Service" or "Service of the Kingdom," and those of personal dedication to service, like "Teach me, my God and King" (H. 476, P. 401) and "Forth in thy Name" (H. 150, P. 406).

149

Section V. The Work of God

Now we arrive at the theological summit of the Old Covenant—
prophecy. We need here a group of hymns that will evoke thoughts
of the work of God. They might be subgrouped as follows:

A. REDEMPTION

    Praise, my soul (H. 282, P. 16)

    Praise to the Holiest (H. 343)

    Triumphant Sion (H. 381)

B. MAN'S APPROACH TO THE DIVINE MAJESTY

    Eternal Light (H. 478)

    Be thou my vision (P. 391)

    Lord of all being (H. 291, P. 89)

Section VI. Thanksgiving for the Work of God

In this section we might include a number of metrical or para-
phrased psalms, like "The Lord's my shepherd" (P. 84) or "Praise
to the Lord, the Almighty" (H. 279, P. 15), and other hymns of
thanksgiving which might be thus subdivided:

A. THE CHURCH'S THANKSGIVING

    Now thank we all our God (H. 276, P. 29)

    Let all the world in ev'ry corner sing (H. 290)

B. FOR PERSONAL PROVIDENCES

    When all thy mercies (H. 297, P. 94)

C. FOR SPIRITUAL BLESSINGS

    King of glory (EH. 424)

D. FOR THE GLORY AND GOODNESS OF GOD

    From all that dwell (H. 277, P. 11)

    Immortal, invisible (H. 301, P. 7)

Up to this point the hymnal has shown hymns whose primary
images are Old Testament images. What they will all have in common will be that they declare a faith, and a sense of sin, which is in
itself not a fully dogmatic Christian faith. Permit me to emphasize
once again that this is no discredit to these hymns. All that could be
said by way of limitation is that a service which included hymns only
from this first part of the collection would not be overtly and creedal-
ly Christian in the fullest sense. But then a service which included
only hymns from the second half might by its overexalted tone fail

to reach down to the spiritual condition of the worshipers. Of course, the assumption here is that the reading of the Old and New Testaments in public worship is for exactly the same reason obligatory. People who come to church off the street (the dusty and congested street, or the lonely and barren street) cannot begin their worship at the top of the mountain; they need symbolically to be led once again through the great story of salvation, and reminded that when God loved the world, what he loved was what they are familiar with. Some enthusiasts criticize such hymns as we would include in our first half on the ground of being "unitarian." That misses their point. The use of such hymns, and of psalms and Old Testament readings, alongside hymns of specifically Christian doctrine with Christology as their center is an act of compassion toward the Christian whose pilgrimage is no more straightforward or innocent than was that of the children of Israel.

New Testament Images

But with what a sense of drama and expectancy one now encounters the season of Advent. This section may be preceded by one or two hymns of a "gospel call" character like "The Lord is rich and merciful" (P. 328)—a singularly felicitous choice, because of the ambiguity with which, having sung "Lord" meaning "God the Father," one finds in the end that one has been singing it as meaning "Christ." (Never neglect the hymns of this author, T. T. Lynch! They often have a bad line or two, but they are at their best deeply suggestive of Christian things.)

In the Advent section we include hymns of expectation of the gospel—hymns again recalling the world's need.

Hark! the glad sound! (H. 7)

O come, O come, Emmanuel (H. 2, P. 110)

Come, thou long-expected Jesus (H. 1, P. 103)

The Christmas section may be strengthened perhaps by the addition of one or two hymns expressing the "self emptying" of Philippians 2, like "One who is all unfit to count" (P. 330).

The Epiphany would require a subsection, expressing the effect of the incarnation on the whole of mankind and the offerings that mankind brings to the Savior. The pattern here is set by "Hail to the Lord's Anointed" (H. 545, P. 105).

151

Then what must we do? We must keep to the pattern of the Gospels if we are committed to this biblical pattern, but this may upset the order which the Church Year would naturally demand. As the creation is followed by the fall in the Old Testament, so the incarnation is followed in Matthew and Luke at once by the baptism and the temptation. The juxtaposition of the temptation and the incarnation has much to commend it in a hymnal. But unhappily the hymn writers have not very successfully met the need for hymns on this subject, or on the baptism of Christ. Nor have they given us much on the early years of Christ. But if we find any good hymns on that subject, they ought to come immediately after the Epiphany. I can at present suggest G. A. Studdert-Kennedy's "Close by the heedless worker's side" (SP. 469), E. R. Conder's "Ye fair green hills of Galilee" (CP. 106), and Charles Wesley's "Servant of all" (MHB. 575; see Appendix B, pp. 189-90).

The only hymns on the baptism are those associated with John the Baptist, such as "On Jordan's bank" (H. 10, P. 115), but these usually miss the Gospel significance of the event. Let the hymn writers get busy at this point. On the temptation there is, of course, "Forty days and forty nights" (H. 55, P. 148), and a thoroughly uninspiring piece of writing it is. Far better is Watts's "With joy we meditate the grace" (CP. 97). There are of course many hymns associated with the season of Lent, but the center of these is usually penitence, fasting, and discipline, which have their place elsewhere.

On the ministry of Christ there are again few good hymns, and we want far more. Here are a few examples of hymns which celebrate it well: "O Master Workman" (P. 412), "O love, how deep, how broad" (H. 344, P. 150) [if not in the preceding section]. Certain hymns are then needed which especially refer to Gospel incidents, such as the healing of the sick in "At even ere the sun was set" (H. 168, P. 55) and any other incidents on which good hymns can be found. Hymns like "Thou art the Way" (H. 361) could follow in a section headed "Response to the Life and Teaching of Christ."

Then we follow the great drama to its conclusion by moving on to hymns on the passion and the resurrection. Among the resurrection hymns can be included the best of the hymns written for "Sunday morning" and the best of those with a "springtime" note. The ascension must follow at once, and it may include a variety of hymns on this exalted and many-sided subject, not forgetting "And have the bright immensities" (H. 354). Still following the story we come to Pentecost, and here it will be well to group together the hymns which refer specifically to the events of Acts 2:1-11 (of which very few at present appear in American hymnals), and then perhaps to go straight on to a larger section of "The Gifts of the Spirit," which will not only find a place for many well-known hymns but will provide a convenient bridge to the last section of the book, which would deal with the experience of the church and of the believer.

The sacraments must be kept as close as possible to the gospel. But they properly come in that section which corresponds to the Epistles.

Then should perhaps come those hymns which deal with the church's corporate response to the gospel commands: hymns of the church's fellowship, privileges, worship, and militant work in the world. (This is where we put the hymns usually relegated to "Missions.") Then at once a good section of hymns expressing the Christian's personal thanksgiving and commitment to Christ—where Watts and Wesley and the other classic writers would have their special contribution to make. All the great hymns in praise of Christ would come here. This could be followed by a section called "The New Commandment" and including hymns commonly headed "Faith and Courage," or with some such title.

The commemoration of individual saints ought also to come somewhere near here, since saints for whom hymns are written are commonly New Testament figures.

But finally we must deal with "Eternal Life" in its various aspects, picking up the deep notes sounded in the First Epistle of John and the last discourses in John's Gospel.

> Love divine, all loves excelling (H. 479, P. 228)
>
> The God of Abraham praise (H. 285, *not* P. 14: see above, p. 110)
>
> Ye watchers and ye holy ones (H. 599, P. 30)

Eternal life as promised now, and eternal life as pictured in the world to come, can be closely associated here, and the section will lead at once to a section on "The Last Judgment," and perhaps (if this be not too bold) a very last section on "The Eternal Mystery" —the Holy Trinity—so that the hymn which appears first in so many books, "Holy, Holy, Holy," will appear almost last here. But this is right, for the doctrine of the Blessed Trinity is a projection from the New Testament which the church accepts but which comes after all that is said in the Scriptures.

Not further to tire the reader we will only add a few brief notes. I believe that it is possible to say that a hymn which did not find a place in this scheme was probably a fairly useless hymn. Various familiar sections are not mentioned, of course. "Harvest," for example. There is no reason why harvest hymns should not come under "Creation," or under "Providence" or possibly under "Judgment." "Marriage"? If a marriage hymn is not fit to place in the section on Christian commitment, it need not be included. "Morning" and "Evening"? Most certainly if any hymn on these subjects has no more to say than that it is morning or evening, then it is not fit to sing and should be discarded. Hymns of such reference should be put where their real subjects dictate—"Providence," "The Trinity," "Thanksgiving," "Creation."

One exception to this rule could perhaps be made. There are some hymns which really have little musical or literary merit and yet provide friendly songs, for the purpose of what one might call "morale raising." Some of them are hardly Christian at all; some of them will not last much longer. A section of "Christian Community Songs" might not be entirely out of place. I do not propose to suggest here what ought to be included there, but if it is true, as I believe, that a hymn can, without being very well argued or beautifully written, nonetheless have an image that a congregation finds profitable, then perhaps it should be included even though its subject matter is too thin to be relevant to a section in the body of the book.

But all this is merely to arouse thought. Even if it arouses exasperated opposition, it will not have been a waste of time. Let me repeat the assumptions: They are that hymns are more than a mere adornment of the service; that used and read and chosen as positive statements and the bearers of powerful images they can do enormous good; and that the rational deployment of the material is likely to make the proper use of the hymnal easier and its trivial use more difficult for those into whose hands it will fall.

8. Hymns for Tomorrow

A Dissent from Conservative Values

Two questions now remain to be dealt with. Both concern the direction which hymnody ought to take if it is to be a fit adornment for relevant and vital Christianity in the second half of the twentieth century. But they need to be kept separate.

These are they: At what points do our hymns, as presently used, tend to preserve irreligious and sentimental values? What new kinds of hymnody may best serve the new age upon which we are now entering?

I have done my best to indicate by a few examples certain tendencies in our hymn singing which I believe to be deplorable but also curable. The choosing of hymns by habit instead of by the free and firm use of intelligence is one. The stupid and inattentive singing of hymns is another. The encouragement of congregations to believe in their right never to learn anything new is a third. All these things tend to the preservation of supinely conservative values, and conservative values have no place in a church which is engaged in a pilgrimage. Conservative values are adequately represented in Num. 11:5: "We remember the fish, which we did eat in Egypt freely." Preparation for the hymnody of the next generation should therefore be undertaken in a spirit of militant and radical reformation. Many familiar things had better go, but many treasures thoughtlessly discarded ought to return. And above all, what takes place in the minds and decisions of editors should be based not on conservative expediency but on a conviction of what the present day and the immediate future needs.

In many ways I believe that the United States has much to teach Britain in this matter. Such a hymnal as the *Hymnal for Colleges and Schools* (1956) shows the kind of critical standard which ought to be regarded as necessary nowadays, especially in a book designed for young people. The nearest to this in an English hymnbook is probably *The BBC Hymn Book* of 1951. There is no need for a modern hymnal to be precious, highbrow, unpractical, or too learned for popular singing. All that is needed is that the dead wood be more ruthlessly cut away than it is at present. Rather less attention ought to be paid to what editors believe to be the wishes of the in-attentive and careless among our worshipers. It is often surprising to what an extent this power of the careless is overestimated, and to what a small extent material put into a hymnbook for the sake of "giving ground" in that direction is left unused in places where the work of the church is being most vigorously done.

All this has been said before, but it must be repeated until there is a general evidence that it is being attended to. The new hymn-books must make intelligent and convinced religion easy to express, and superstitious and silly religion difficult to express.

A New Hymns in the Old Style

Our other question is more positive and makes higher demands. To repair what is defective in present religion is one necessity: to communicate the faith to a generation whose ideas have been revolutionized by social change is another.

At the present time a great deal more is being done in music than in the writing of words. Elsewhere I shall be dealing with these musical developments, which are truly dramatic. Here I must be content to ask how much is being done to provide new words and new styles of hymnody for a new generation.

People are still writing hymns—there is no doubt of that. The Hymn Society of America manages to elicit a good deal of literature from those who respond to its demands for new hymnody on certain subjects. But where is anybody writing a hymn that really answers the profound needs of today?

It is—and we may take comfort in this—not only a matter of

how many new hymns we can find, but also of how much we can find in the older literature that will speak with a new freshness now. It is this older literature that I believe is going to help us most.

Now there are certain authors who have written hymns of a traditional kind, using modern words and modern images. We mentioned one (p. 83) that talked of buses and steam engines, and we said that it was in danger of an untimely end to its useful life because of the advent of electric lamps and diesel locomotives. The contribution of Thomas Tiplady to this kind of literature is actually a good deal more impressive. Tiplady's hymns are known better in the United States than they are in Britain outside his immediate circle. They were all written for use at a downtown mission in London where he worked for twenty-three years (the Lambeth Mission), and where the evening congregation tended to consist of people who had no religious background at all. He was heard to say that it was usually necessary to ask the congregation to extinguish their cigarettes while they were in the sanctuary. His language was never very original and the thought forms were wholly traditional, but he managed always to avoid awkward or recondite images, and at his best he is very good indeed. There is a carol-like simplicity about the manner in which great thoughts are simply expressed in the following lines:

> All ye who know that on the Cross
>   Christ did salvation bring,
> Lift up your heart, lift up your voice
>   And make the whole world ring.
>
> O make the whole world ring with joy
>   And spread the news around:
> Till every man shall hear the song
>   That we in Christ have found.
>
> The song of our redemption raise
>   And storm high heaven's gate,
> Till angels in amaze look out
>   At man's exalted state.
>
> For we, the fallen, now may rise
>   And stand with Christ on high,

> In robes made white beneath his cross
> And "Hallelujah" cry.[1]

Tiplady writes in a traditional style; his concession to the unsophisticated mind of his congregation is in the use of very simple and clear images. He will still use a word like "cry" for "shout," which is a conventional archaism. But his hymns have made a great impact on his congregation, and they emerge from a specific and local need, which is the authentic origin of many of our finest hymns. These hymns are not well known in Britain outside Tiplady's constituency, but they are much sung by the Baptists and the Disciples of Christ in the United States and four of them are in *The Hymnal* of the Episcopal Church in Canada.

Another author of the "traditional" kind who succeeded excellently in writing simple and persuasive material for our time was the late G. W. Briggs. I believe that the greatest of his hymns was one of the last—possibly the very last—that he ever wrote. It is a hymn on that subject where good hymns are so much needed—the ministry of Christ:

> Jesus, whose all-redeeming love
>   No penitent did scorn,
> Who didst the stain of guilt remove
>   Till hope anew was born:
>
> To thee, Physician of the soul,
>   The lost, the outcast came:
> Thou didst restore and make them whole,
>   Disburdened of their shame.
>
> 'Twas love, thy love, their bondage broke,
>   Whose fetters sin had bound;
> For faith to love did answer make
>   And free forgiveness found.
>
> Thou didst rebuke the scornful pride
>   That called thee "sinners' friend,"

[1] *100 New Hymns of Praise* (London: Featherstone Press, n.d.), No. 21, sts. 1-4.

Thy mercy as thy Father's wide,
God's mercy without end.

Along life's desecrated way
Where man despairing trod,
Thy love all-pitying did display
The pitying love of God.

Jesus, that pardoning grace to find
I too would come to thee:
O merciful to all mankind,
Be merciful to me.[2]

That kind of material, unspectacular and innocent but sound and honest, can add much to the virility of a modern hymnbook, and will appeal to those whose tastes are traditional without assenting to any unwillingness to be surprised. Other authors are doing the same kind of thing, and on the whole one can find some good "traditional" material by contemporary authors in almost any current hymnal. There is not very much of it at a high standard, but the stream is not dry.

A New Vocabulary

However, it is possible to move a good deal further than this, and here there are two suggestions one could make at once. In the first place, the reader will probably know what a revolution in taste among hymn singers was achieved by the action of Percy Dearmer (for Anglicans) and W. Garrett Horder (for Dissenters) in Britain in including in their hymnals a little of the work of the seventeenth-century poets who were not hymn wrters. Dearmer did it first in *The English Hymnal* and later in *Songs of Praise:* Horder did it in his *Worship Song* (1905). A few poems like George Herbert's "Teach me, my God and King" (H. 476, P. 401) and Henry Vaughan's "My soul, there is a country" (SP. 585) came into currency as hymns, to the lasting benefit of the singers. This was not the first experiment of the kind. John Wesley had used some of George Herbert's hymns, drastically rewritten, in his hymnbooks,

[2] *Hymns of the Faith* (London: Oxford University Press, 1956), No. 53.

159

and another experiment on a larger scale was made in a little-known book edited by John Gambold in 1754, called *Collection of Hymns*, in which he used a number of poems by Herbert, John Donne, and Richard Crashaw. Dearmer's intention was probably mere directly didactic than either Wesley's or Gambold's, inasmuch as he was preparing, in *Songs of Praise*, a hymnbook for schools which should introduce young listeners not only to great hymns and tunes but also to great literature (which the familiar hymns sometimes, in his view, failed to do).

Now the real question we want to ask here is a curious one, but to put it thus is to expose the heart of the problem. How do you write hymns today which will be great hymns tomorrow? That is what we really want to know. The answer must come in three propositions: (*a*) you cannot write a "great" hymn, in this sense, to order: you can only do your best; (*b*) a great hymn can be interpreted as a hymn which a very large number of Christians come to know and love; (*c*) but a great hymn can also be a hymn which is an illuminating expression of Christian faith even though few people have recognized it as such.

If you take two hymns of Isaac Watts which originally appeared in the third book of his *Hymns and Spiritual Songs*, the whole of which is devoted to the theme of the Lord's Supper, you see the difference between "great" in our two senses. "When I survey the wondrous cross" is a great hymn in the first sense. "Nature with open volume" is a great hymn in the second.

The truth is that Isaac Watts did not know which of his hymns would turn out to be "great" in the first sense. He could not have told that "When I survey" would catch the imagination of the Christian world, and that "Nature with open volume" would not. Charles Wesley had no idea that "Hark, how all the welkin rings," altered by Martin Madan to "Hark, the herald angels sing," would sweep round the world, while two centuries after its composition "See how great a flame aspires" would still be sung only by English Methodists.

So how can a hymn writer of today tell whether his hymn will be a great hymn tomorrow? My own view is that he will be wise to try to discover what it is that makes the unknown-great hymns great, and correspondingly unwise to try to see what has made the famous-great hymns popular. To try to cultivate popularity is always to cheapen art. To cultivate integrity is to renounce the right to judge one's work on posterity's behalf: and that right must always be renounced. There is a pregnant text (Deut. 29:29) which artists as well as moralists can profit by: "The secret things belong unto the Lord our God; but those things which are revealed belong unto us and to our children for ever, that we may do all the words of this law." The "secret things" include what tomorrow is going to make of today's hymns. What is this "law"?

It is an authentic obedience to the light that is given. How in fact is this law obeyed in a great piece of hymn writing? Let us again look at the full text of "Nature with open volume," a hymn which very few people know, but which surely can be called "great."

> Nature with open volume stands
>   To spread her Maker's praise abroad;
> And every labour of His hands
>   Shows something worthy of a God.
>
> But in the grace that rescued man,
>   His brightest form of glory shines;
> Here on the cross 'tis fairest drawn
>   In precious blood and crimson lines.
>
> Here His whole Name appears complete,
>   Nor wit can guess, nor reason prove
> Which of the letters best is writ,
>   The power, the wisdom, or the love.
>
> Here I behold his inmost heart
>   Where grace and vengeance strangely join,
> Piercing his Son with sharpest smart
>   To make the purchas'd pleasures mine.
>
> O the sweet wonders of that cross
>   Where Christ my Saviour loved and died!*
> Her noblest life my spirit draws
>   From His dear wounds and bleeding side.
>
>   [* originally "Where God the Saviour . . ."]

161

I would for ever speak His Name
In sounds to mortal ears unknown,
With angels join to praise the Lamb
And worship at His Father's throne (see p. 66).

We have already indicated why this hymn is not popular as "When I survey" is popular. It lacks the initial and evident attractiveness of the better-known hymn. But we call it "great" because of three things, of which the first two are obvious enough. In the first place, it deals with a profound theological issue, which means a profound truth of human experience in the context of ultimate reality. That truth is the relation between *nature* and *grace*. It points out the contrast carefully and emphatically in its first and second verses. It leads the singer from the flat land of reason to the heights of devotional experience, the emotional pressure rising all the way from the beginning to the end. This is another way in which it differs from "When I survey"; the better-known hymn is "warm" all the way. "Nature with open volume" begins "cool."

Secondly, it deals very much in Watts's neat and epigrammatic way of expressing great truths. The second couplet of the third stanza is the supreme example. When the greatest things are as simply expressed as this, without any blunting of the cutting edge of their truth, you have great hymn writing.

Those, I say, are enough obvious considerations, and keeping them in view the hymn writer can feel reasonably safe if he sets out to write a hymn which deals with the great matters of our faith, and if he can bring reason and emotion together without confusion, using language which mingles profundity, sincerity, sonorousness, and simplicity. But if he does this, he may still fail to write a great hymn. (He may fail anyhow; it is not his to judge: but there is another matter which he must not ignore.)

The third point, then, comes of asking whether Isaac Watts had any business at all writing that fourth stanza—the verse which even those hymnals which print the hymn at all are shy of. Few will have read the hymn carefully (of those who have not considered it before) without having a feeling that that verse spoils it, with its appalling image of the Father punishing the Son. It is almost repellent. It expresses a mythology which perhaps many people now find quite alien to their Christian thinking.

I do not here judge whether that verse ought to be sung in our present age. Probably we are right not to ask congregations to sing it in the unpremediated state in which congregations nowadays come to their hymn singing. Perhaps in the end it is a bad verse. But I hear in that verse the note of faith—faith in the sense of *risk*. I mean this in the poet's sense, not merely in the theologian's. To a modern ear, those lines represent Watts writing down what he hardly dare write down. It does not matter if to Watts it was a commonplace sentiment. As it stands, for today, it is a dangerous one. The danger is of a special and valuable sort.

What makes so much hymn writing useless and demoralizing is its complete divorcement from the real stuff of common life. There is something so desperately safe about it that it cannot bear any resemblance to life as the Christian knows it must be lived. Life, for the Christian (for anybody—but the Christian has the advantage of being able to see this clearly in the teachings of Christ), is not an aggregation of days but a series of crises and decisions. There are occasions on the battlefield when a man must decide in a situation in which his action, if it succeeds, will get him the Victoria Cross, and if it fails, will get him shot. Most acts of daring which come up as occasions for decorations of valor are acts which, had they misfired, might have landed their agents in prison at least. The Good Samaritan story is the story of a situation in which one was absolutely obliged to be either a miserable coward or a conspicuous hero. Nobody could be neutral about the man lying by the roadside. Either you ignored him and were a coward, or you helped him and were a saint. The story is told so that Christians can see that life essentially is much more like that than people usually realize. Parables of judgment and crisis abound for exactly the same reason. They tell of situations in which you cannot be neutral; in which nonaction is a kind of action.

The ethical implications of this are not our subject. Our subject here is the artist's interpretation of what Paul Tillich has called so memorably "the courage to be." In a world at odds with God and with reality, there must be crisis and tension, and the *good* action is never the *safe* action. Therefore in any work of art, and a hymn is a form of art, the artist must often do things (that is, in hymns, write things) which are *almost* terrible, of which posterity, the only capable judge, *may* say, "That is bad," or even, "That is blasphemous." If the action "comes off" the artist gets the accolade of greatness. If it does not, he is disgraced. These lines of Isaac Watts are just a single example of that—we do not altogether know yet whether they are a blasphemy or a glory. Much of Isaac Watts is mere carpentry, mere hackwork, blameless when it is adequate, ridiculous when it turns out to misfire. This is not in that category. It is not like the lines

> Abram, I'll be thy God, said he,
> And he was Abram's God.

It is certainly true that the greatness of the evangelical hymn writers was in their capacity to take great risks with their writing. The greatness of Charles Wesley is in those lines which successfully and with flashing illumination express the great verities of the Christian faith; and it is there no less because there are lines very like these great ones which say the same things with appalling bathos and crudity. It is where you have a hymn writer who will in the end commit himself utterly to the expression of the ineffable, hoping that poetry will bridge the gulf between reason and reality:

> Where reason fails with all her powers,
> There faith prevails, and love adores.

That is Isaac Watts again (the last couplet of "We give immortal praise," CP. 220). Reason does fail in communicating the faith; poetry is the only alternative. The writer who can crash resoundingly and ludicrously is so often the writer who in his great moment can get through to the heart of reality.

This is what we simply do not see nowadays in the demure and careful hymn writing that comes from the poets of the congregations. People will write "home and family hymns" by the dozen without ever indicating that they have reckoned with the anthropological unnaturalness of the bourgeois Western family. People will write hymns of social service without showing any knowledge of the fact that saying "I'll help you" could be an outrageous insult to a person's privacy. People still write missionary hymns as if they did not know that Ghana sends students to Western universities who get doctorates and return to be nationalists. People write hymns for youth which make no mention of sex, and treat all Christian youth as though they were novices in monasteries and nunneries. And when it comes to dealing with the immensities of the incarnation and the atonement, who today is there who writes hymns that convey anything of the cosmic counterpoint of a book like Martin Versfield's *A Mirror of Philosophers?* Who today writes with the sense of awe and the tongue of fire that possessed the classic evangelicals? If we don't now want the "slaughtered Lamb," we certainly don't want to be left with "he died to make us good."

Irony

Now this is the point at which it is worth while to note that in our time a certain kind of communication has taken a firm hold on our own people—irony and satire. Irony is nowadays very far from the church's speech. But it need not be far from hymn writing.

It is certainly not far from the speech of the carols. I advocate a return to the carol in our public praise as a first step to good hymn writing. The reader may care again to look at the carol "Tomorrow shall be my dancing day" (pp. 180-81) and perhaps at some of the others mentioned on pp. 65-76 of my book *The English Carol* [3] and to consider again how the ballad carols juxtaposed theological ideas which seem incompatible to the modern mind. Especially did they juxapose the passion and *laughter,* redemption and the *dance,* atonement and a *love song.* It was the special genius of those ancient ages to make these bold collocations of ideas which Protestantism normally separates. What makes our contemporary church literature mournful is its obstinate insistence on conventional associations of ideas. It was this, of course, which provoked the reaction of Percy Dearmer in *Songs of Praise. Songs of Praise* was the work in hymnology of the man who was also working on the *Oxford Book of Carols*—a man who wanted hymns to sound more like carols.

In our own time the children of a sophisticated and intellectual age are impatient of the conventionality of church language, of the

---

[3] New York: Oxford University Press, 1958.

absence of anything *new,* any unexpected collocation of ideas; and although the skeptic does not so express it, what he means is that our modern hymnody and church habits do not express the incarnation, the scandal and the miracle of Godhead taking human flesh.

This seems to be the fundamental point, and it is from the carols that we can best learn. There are certain technical points which, as I believe, can be looked at by modern authors as possible helps to a fresh style in writing. Rhyme and meter are among these.

Are Meter and Rhyme Necessary?

In the second place, there is a technical point which we might suggest. Part of the "conventional style" of hymns is due to the custom of writing them in strict meter and in rhyming verses. It is time now to reexamine the necessity of this style. Strict meter is really the legacy of the old Psalters. The carols were never in strict meter —odd added syllables or elided syllables are constantly found in their lines. They present difficulty in singing only when the singer insists on being self-conscious and consequently inattentive to what he is singing. The carefree singing that one hears at Christmastime makes light of the inequalities in "The first Noel," and although "O come, all ye faithful" is not a carol, it is the most famous example of an "irregular" hymn, written in rhythmic prose without rhyme. So far from being thought difficult or esoteric it is surely among every Christian's "top twenty."

As for rhyme, this is an old lyric device which makes for music in read words, and it had, in the old Psalters, the added advantage of making couplets easy to memorize when congregations sang so largely by dictation. But it does restrict the vocabulary of hymns, and it leads their writers into all manner of cliché. It is the source, for example, of Tiplady's "cry." It often produces a weak last line in which a writer finds it desperately necessary to "find his way home" by way of a "heaven" to rhyme with "given." One might add that it sometimes produces a disaster in sound when a pronunciation has changed, so that "praises" or "faces" has to rhyme with "Jesus"— tolerable in the eighteenth century but uncomfortable in our own.

A touch of freedom will probably make all the difference to our modern hymns. An example of clever rhyme (indeed a single rhyme running all through the hymn) united with free rhythm produces one of the most delightful of modern hymns on the promises of heaven, "I would choose to be a doorkeeper in the house of the Lord," of which these are stanzas 1 and 3:

> I would choose to be a doorkeeper
>   In the House of the Lord
> Rather than lords and ladies
>   In satin on the sward.
> To draw the bolts for the white souls
>   Would be my rich reward:
> And I the happy doorkeeper
>   To the House of the Lord.
>
> They come with shining faces
>   To the House of the Lord;
> The broken hearts and weary
>   That life has racked and scored:
> They come hurrying and singing
>   To sit down at his board,
> They are young and they are joyful
>   In the house of the Lord (SP. 196).

Dignity gives place here to a springing energy, and the rhyme provides a kind of groundbass.

There are very few examples at present of hymns written without rhyme. An experiment in assonance was quoted above (p. 81); but here is one which shows how a well-known meter lends itself to the use of unrhymed lines without any sense of incompleteness. The meter here is strict, and the vocabulary a little recondite for everyday use: but the hymn was written for a theological seminary by its principal about thirty years ago, and in that context it is beautiful and appropriate.

> Holy, eternal Son of God, the Dayspring,
> Pierced once and passion'd on the Rood to save us,
> First-born of many brethren, strong Redeemer,
>   Lord of the harvest,
>
> Thou who hast called us, not of our deserving,
> Heralds and stewards of the heavenly treasure,

Grant thine assoiling, from on high anoint us,
Vowed to thy service.

Succour our brethren who are gone before us;
Shield them in danger of the flesh or spirit;
Lonely, disheartened, reft of strength and burdened,
Cheer and sustain them.

Vouchsafe thy servants the prophetic vision,
Soundness of learning, apostolic fervour;
Grant perseverance, and at our departing,
Saviour, receive us.[4]

This is another hymn that grew out of a local need, and one of the means through which a revival in hymnody may well be achieved is the encouragement of such local hymn writing. Nine tenths of it may turn out to be useful only in the place where it is written. But one or two immortals may thus be born. The official hymnary need not be an extinguisher of all inspiration. And the custom so widely prevalent in the United States of using printed service sheets in public worship gives excellent opportunity for the occasional printing and singing of a new local hymn. The tyranny of meter and rhyme are joined by the tyranny of the official hymnary in impeding the free flow of good contemporary hymnody. A vital local congregation might well look for inspiration in its members and encourage it: but this would only happen if people are prepared to be satisfied with this limited constituency for their hymns, and do not have ambitions of joining the immortals. Seats in heaven are not theirs to seek. The service of their immediate neighbor ought to be sufficient ambition: that, at least, seems to be the teaching of the Gospels on such matters.

Some Local Experiments

Now if one adds together these ingredients of a new hymnody—a breakaway from traditional notions of style, a new exploitation of irony, and the need of a new situation—what happens can be exem-

[4] Nathaniel Micklem, Principal of Mansfield College, Oxford, 1932-53; in *A Gallimaufry* (Nashville: Parthenon Press, 1954). Also in a MS collection of hymns used at Mansfield College. Used by permission of author.

plified from certain recent developments in England. A break-through is certainly on the way. It has already come in music. From Olivier Messiaen to Geoffrey Beaumont, European composers are throwing overboard the traditional ideas about church music: and similar things are happening in the United States. This is where the hymn writer should look for his ideas, and in England there is one writer whose work has begun to give signs that all is not lost. He is Sydney Carter, and his name is not yet well known, although some of his songs have been sung by the celebrated entertainer Donald Swann.

Carter has composed a number of songs on religious subjects, of which I will quote one here. It is a carol based on the same idea that is in "Tomorrow shall be my dancing day," and he has set it to an adaptation of an old Shaker tune. What, think you, has this to say to our aspirations toward a new hymnody?

> I danced in the morning when the world was begun,
> And I danced in the moon and the stars and the sun,
> And I came down from heaven and danced on the earth:
> At Bethlehem I had my birth.
>
> > Dance then wherever you may be,
> > I am Lord of the dance, said he;
> > I'll lead you all, wherever you may be,
> > I will lead you all in the dance, said he.
>
> I danced for the scribe and the Pharisee,
> But they would not dance, and they wouldn't follow me,
> I danced for the fishermen, for James and John—
> They came with me and the dance went on.
> > Dance then. . . .
>
> I danced on the Sabbath and I cured the lame,
> And the holy people said it was a shame.
> They whipped and stripped and they hung me high
> And they left me there on a cross to die.
> > Dance then. . . .
>
> I danced on a Friday when the sky turned black,
> It's hard to dance with the devil on your back.

> They buried my body and they thought I'd gone,
> But I am the dance and I still go on.
> Dance then. . . .[5]

In Britain a profound impression has been made by a mime drama for television called *A Man Dies*. It was devised by Ernest Marvin, a Presbyterian minister, in the city of Bristol, for performance by a group of adolescents who attend the youth club at his church. There is little dialogue in the play, but there is much music. Part of the music is provided by two long songs, sung in sections at different parts of the play by a girl "pop singer," to an accompaniment of a dance band of a primitive kind. The performance needs to be violent and vulgar, since it is accompanying at the same time a mime of the ministry of Christ (seen on a raised stage behind) and a large group of twist dancers who are dancing all the time in the center of the stage. Now and again the central figures of the drama come down and interrupt or pass through the dancers. The monstrous irony of the world's rejection of Christ is built up to a trenchant climax. Now while this is going on, these songs are being sung. One is called "Gentle Christ," the other, "Go it Alone." I will quote a few stanzas of both.

> Gentle Christ, wise and good,
> We nailed him to a cross of wood.
> The Son of God, he lived to save,
> In borrowed stable and borrowed grave.
>
> When he walked into the shopping street
> We threw spring flowers before his feet,
> Glad to get an excuse to shout,
> No need to worry what you shout about.
> Gentle Christ . . . .
>
> They say as many would say today
> "We wouldn't have treated our Saviour that way"
> But Gentle Christ, wise and good,
> They nailed him to a cross of wood.
> Gentle Christ . . . .

[5] *9 Ballads or Carols* (London, Clarion Photographic Agency, 1964). Used by permission of author.

Soldiers came at Pilate's call
Led him into the common hall,
Took sharp thorns and made a crown,
Dressed him in a scarlet gown.
  Gentle Christ . . . .

At last they came to the hanging place
A hill we call the Eyeless Face,
They gave him drugs to kill the pain,
He pushed the cup away again.
  Gentle Christ . . . .

  Go it alone, Go it alone,
  There was no need to go it alone!

We weren't sure we could do what he said,
We felt like children away from home,
Till we trusted his power and remembered his words,
And we didn't have to go it alone.
  Go it alone. . . .

You know how it is when you've walked for miles,
How your feet get rubbed and raw to the bone?
Well, we were like that, but our hearts were on fire
For we didn't have to go it alone!
  Go it alone . . . .

You know at the death of a person you love,
How your heart hits the floor and you're on your own?
Well, we suddenly felt he was at our side,
And we didn't have to go it alone
  Go it alone . . . .

Some are lonely and suffer in hospital beds,
Where the world goes by without hearing their groan;
Some are killed on the roads by drunken fools—
But they don't have to go it alone.
  Go it alone. . . .[6]

[6] Both lyrics used with acknowledgments to the publisher Ivy Music Limited, 10 Denmark Street, London W. C. 2.

The fact that these songs (in which there are many more verses than are quoted here) are immediately related to their context and perhaps would sound strange without it reinforces all that we have said about hymns. The drama of worship is now being seen with new eyes all over Christendom. These new eyes will have new ears behind them, and for these new ears we need a new music and a new hymnody. Of one thing there can be no doubt: the writer of those lines knows how to use images and how to lay modern life straight on to the pattern of the life of Christ.

The popularizers are giving a lead. What Ira D. Sankey did in his day for the unchurched poor, these people are doing for the unchurched "welfare staters." The "squares" are lagging behind; there is little of this vitality, this irony, this concern, to be seen in what they are writing. What we need now is for a few poets of acknowledged standing and skill to take the risk of dirtying their hands with the common stuff of popular piety and see the necessity of providing us with a new hymnody. If, as I myself firmly believe, the new hymns turn out to be carols rather than hymns, earthy, familiar, bold, and by present-day standards unconventional, so much the better. Not only will the new hymns produce a new and daring faith. They will shed new light on the old hymns. We shall not lose the Old Hundredth and "O worship the King"; but we may start singing them without that glazed expression and that mental stagnation which are now only too familiar. If the first Reformation was born in song, the new Reformation (without which religion as we know it could perish from the earth) will be similarly born. There is just time: only just time.

Appendix A
An Experimental Table of Contents

PART I

1. God the Creator
    a. God the Maker of All Things
    b. Man's Search for Knowledge of Nature
2. Man's Fall and God's Promise of Forgiveness
3. Pilgrimage
    a. God's Relevation of Himself in the Moral Law
    b. The Pilgrimage of Life
4. Human Relations and Service
    a. The Nation
    b. Social Service
    c. Personal Service
5. The Work and Promises of God
    a. Redemption
    b. Man's Approach to the Divine Majesty
6. Thanksgiving for God's Work and Promises
    a. The Church's Thanksgiving
    b. For Personal and Corporate Providences
    c. For Spiritual Blessings
    d. For the Glory of God Revealed

PART II

1. The Gospel Call
2. The Life, Death, Resurrection, and Ascension of Christ
    a. His Advent
    b. His Incarnation
    c. His Manifestation
    d. His Temptation
    e. His Ministry
    f. His Passion
    g. His Resurrection
    h. His Ascension and Reign

3. The Holy Spirit
   a. The Coming of the Holy Spirit
   b. The Gifts of the Holy Spirit
4. The Church of God
   a. The Sacraments: Baptism and Communion
   b. The Church's Fellowship and Privileges
   c. The Church's Worship and Intercession
   d. The Church's Work in the World
   e. The Church Triumphant [including commemoration of saints]
5. The Christian's Commitment and Discipleship
   a. Christian Penitence and Prayer
   b. Christian Joy
   c. Christian Hope
6. Eternal Life
   a. The Promise Realized
   b. The Promise Hereafter
   c. The Last Judgment
7. The Blessed Trinity

Possible allocation of hymns normally found in special sections.
   "Morning," "Evening," and "Children's Hymns"—allocated according to subjects.
   "Marriage": if hymns of intercession: II, 4, c.
                if hymns of thanksgiving: I, 6, b.
                if hymns of invocation: II, 3, b.
   "Burial": II, 6, b.
   "Harvest": I, 1, a.
   "Thanksgiving Day": I, 4, a or I, 6, a.

Appendix B
Selected Hymns

1

Isaac Watts's paraphrase of the twenty-third Psalm (see p. 28).

> My Shepherd will supply my need,
>   Jehovah is His name;
> In pastures fresh He makes me feed
>   Beside the living stream.
>
> He brings my wandering spirit back
>   When I forsake His ways,
> And leads me, for His mercy's sake,
>   In paths of truth and grace.
>
> When I walk through the shades of death
>   Thy presence is my stay;
> A word of Thy supporting breath
>   Drives all my fears away.
>
> Thy hand, in sight of all my foes,
>   Doth still my table spread;
> My cup with blessings overflows,
>   Thine oil anoints my head.
>
> The sure provisions of my God
>   Attend me all my days;
> O may Thy house be mine abode,
>   And all my work be praise!
>
> There would I find a settled rest,
>   While others go and come;
> No more a stranger or a guest,
>   But like a child at home (CP. 50).

2

A Hymn by Thomas Binney on the mystery of God's Being and the advocacy of the Holy Spirit (see p. 35).

Eternal Light, eternal Light!
　　How pure the soul must be,
When, placed within Thy searching sight,
It shrinks not, but with calm delight
　　Can live and look on Thee.

The spirits that surround Thy throne
　　May bear the burning bliss;
But that is surely theirs alone,
For they have never, never known
　　A fallen world like this.

O how shall I, whose native sphere
　　Is dark, whose mind is dim,
Before the ineffable appear,
And on my naked spirit bear
　　The uncreated beam?

There is a way for man to rise
　　To that sublime abode:
An offering and a sacrifice,
A Holy Spirit's energies,
　　An Advocate with God.

These, these prepare us for the sight
　　Of holiness above:
The sons of ignorance and night
May dwell in the eternal light
　　Through the eternal love (CP. 21).

3

A hymn by Charles Wesley on Gen. 32:24 and Mark 9:2 ff. (see p. 45).

Shepherd Divine, our wants relieve
　　In this our evil day;
To all Thy tempted followers give
　　The power to watch and pray.

Long as our fiery trials last,
　　Long as the cross we bear,

O let our souls on Thee be cast
   In never-ceasing prayer.

The Spirit of interceding grace
   Give us in faith to claim;
To wrestle till we see Thy Face,
   And know Thy hidden Name.

Till Thou Thy perfect love impart,
   Till Thou Thyself bestow,
Be this the cry of every heart,
   "I will not let Thee go."

I will not let Thee go, unless
   Thou tell Thy Name to me;
With all Thy great Salvation bless,
   And make me all like Thee.

Then let me on the mountain-top
   Behold Thine open Face;
Where faith in sight is swallow'd up,
   And prayer in endless praise (HAM St. 248).

4

Charles Wesley's original version of "Hail the Day that sees Him rise," written in 1739, and preserved unaltered in the 1877 edition of *A Collection of Hymns for the Use of the People Called Methodists*, No. 718 (see p. 52).

Hail the day that sees him rise,
Ravished from our wishful eyes!
Christ, awhile to mortals given,
Reascends his native heaven.

There the pompous triumph waits:
"Lift your heads, eternal gates,
Wide unfold the radiant scene;
Take the King of glory in!"

Circled round with angel-powers,
Their triumphant Lord, and ours,
Conqueror over death and sin,
"Take the King of glory in!"

Him though highest heaven receives,
Still he loves the earth he leaves;

Though returning to his throne,
Still he calls mankind his own.

See, he lifts his hands above!
See, he shows the prints of love!
Hark, his gracious lips bestow
Blessings on his church below!

Still for us his death he pleads,
Prevalent he intercedes;
Near himself prepares our place,
Harbinger of human race.

Master (will we ever say)
Taken from our head to-day,
See thy faithful servants, see,
Ever gazing up to thee.

Grant, though parted from our sight,
High above yon azure height,
Grant our hearts may thither rise,
Following thee beyond the skies.

Ever upward let us move,
Wafted on the wings of love;
Looking when our Lord shall come,
Longing, gasping after home.

There we shall with thee remain,
Partners of thy endless reign;
There thy face unclouded see,
Find our heaven of heavens in thee.

5

"St. Patrick's Breastplate" translated by Mrs. C. F. Alexander (see p. 55).

I bind unto myself to-day
    The strong name of the Trinity,
By invocation of the same,
    The Three in One, and One in Three.

I bind this day to me for ever,
    By power of faith, Christ's Incarnation;
His baptism in Jordan river;
    His death on Cross for my salvation;
His bursting from the spicèd tomb;

His riding up the heavenly way;
His coming at the day of doom;
I bind unto myself to-day.

I bind unto myself to-day
   The virtues of the star-lit heaven,
The glorious sun's life-giving ray,
   The whiteness of the moon at even,
The flashing of the lightning free,
   The whirling wind's tempestuous shocks,
The stable earth, the deep salt sea,
   Around the old eternal rocks.

I bind unto myself to-day
   The power of God to hold and lead,
His eye to watch, his might to stay,
   His ear to hearken to my need.
The wisdom of my God to teach,
   His hand to guide, his shield to ward;
The word of God to give me speech,
   His heavenly host to be my guard.

Christ be with me, Christ within me,
   Christ behind me, Christ before me,
Christ beside me, Christ to win me,
   Christ to comfort and restore me,
Christ beneath me, Christ above me,
   Christ in quiet, Christ in danger,
Christ in hearts of all that love me,
   Christ in mouth of friend and stranger.

I bind unto myself the name,
   The strong name of the Trinity;
By invocation of the same,
   The Three in One, and One in Three,
Of whom all nature hath creation;
   Eternal Father, Spirit, Word:
Praise to the Lord of my salvation,
   Salvation is of Christ the Lord

(abridged, for full version see EH. 212).

6

A Cornish poem of unknown origin and date, which has become well known
as a carol during the past generation. William Sandys' collection of carols
(1833) gives the words and the traditional tune. It appears in the *Oxford
Book of Carols* and in most later comprehensive collections. It was set to music

by **Gustav Holst** for the parish church of Thaxted, Essex. When the **vicar of** Thaxted displayed a copy of the words in his church, his parishioners complained to his bishop and he was ordered to remove this "secular song" from public view. But on being informed that the poem was of sacred origin, the bishop—who perhaps never considered its true meaning—revoked his order. There is an extended reference to it in *The English Carol*, pp. 79-80 (see p. 64).

> Tomorrow shall be my dancing day,
>   I would my true love did so chance
> To see the legend of my play,
>   To call my true love to the dance.
>
>   *Sing O my love, O my love, my love, my
>   love;*
>   *This have I done for my true love.*
>
> Then was I born of a virgin pure,
>   Of her I took my fleshly substance;
> Thus was I knit to man's nature,
>   To call my true love to my dance:
>
> In a manger laid and wrapped I was,
>   So very poor, this was my chance,
> Betwixt an ox and a silly poor ass,
>   To call my true love to my dance:
>
> Then afterwards baptised I was;
>   The Holy Ghost on me did glance,
> My Father's voice heard from above,
>   To call my true love to my dance:
>
> Into the desert I was led,
>   Where I fasted without substance;
> The devil bade me make stones my bread,
>   To have me break my true love's dance:
>
> The Jews on me they made great suit,
>   And with me made great variance,
> Because they loved darkness rather than light,
>   To call my true love to my dance:
>
> For thirty pence Judas me sold,
>   His covetousness for to advance;
> "Mark whom I kiss, the same do hold:
>   The same is he shall lead the dance":
>
> Before Pilate the Jews me brought,
>   Where Barabbas had deliverance;

They scourged me and set me at nought,
  Judged me to die to lead the dance:

Then on the cross I hanged was,
  Where a spear to my heart did glance;
There issued forth both water and blood,
  To call my true love to my dance:

Then down to hell I took my way
  For my true love's deliverance,
And rose again on the third day,
  Up to my true love and the dance:

Then up to heaven I did ascend,
  Where now I dwell in sure substance,
On the right hand of God, that man
  May come unto the general dance.

7

Part of a hymn on the Incarnation and the Passion by Venantius Fortunatus (see p. 65).

Pange lingua gloriosi proelium certaminis.

Sing, my tongue, the glorious battle,
  Sing the ending of the fray;
Now above the cross, the trophy,
  Sound the loud triumphant lay:
Tell how Christ, the world's redeemer,
  As a victim won the day.

Tell how, when at length the fullness
  Of the appointed time was come,
He, the Word, was born of woman,
  Left for us his Fathers' home,
Showed to men the perfect manhood,
  Shone as light amidst the gloom.

Thus, with thirty years accomplished,
  Went he forth from Nazareth,
Destined, dedicate, and willing,
  Wrought his work, and met his death;
Like a lamb he humbly yielded
  On the cross his dying breath.

Faithful cross, thou sign of triumph,
  Now for man the noblest tree,

None in foliage, none in blossom,
  None in fruit thy peer may be;
Symbol of the world's redemption,
  For the weight that hung on thee!

Unto God be praise and glory:
  To the Father and the Son,
To the eternal Spirit, honour
  Now and evermore be done;
Praise and glory in the highest,
    While the timeless ages run (SP 129; for a translation by
      Percy Dearmer and J. M. Neale see EH. 95 and 96).

8

Another hymn on the Passion by Venantius Fortunatus, here abridged and translated by various editors, who based their work on that of J. M. Neale (see pp. 64-65).

Vexilla Regis prodeunt.
The royal banners forward go,
The Cross shines forth in mystic glow,
Where he in flesh, our flesh who made,
Our sentence bore, our ransom paid.

His feet and hands outstretching there,
He will'd the piercing nails to bear,
For us and our redemption's sake
A victim of himself to make.

There whilst he hung, his sacred side
By soldier's spear was opened wide,
To cleanse us in the precious flood
Of water mingled with his blood.

Fulfilled is now what David told
In true prophetic song of old;
To all the nations, "Lo!" saith he,
"Our God is reigning from the tree"
              (for a fuller translation by Neale see EH. 94).

9

A hymn by Prudentius (4th century) translated by R. F. Davis (see pp. 74-75).

Corde natus ex parentis.
Of the Father's heart begotten,
  Ere the world from chaos rose,

He is Alpha: from that Fountain
  All that is and hath been flows;
He is Omega, of all things
  Yet to come the mystic Close,
    Evermore and evermore.

By his word was all created;
  He commanded and 'twas done;
Earth and sky and boundless ocean,
  Universe of three in one,
All that sees the moon's soft radiance,
  All that breathes beneath the sun,

He assumed this mortal body,
  Frail and feeble, doomed to die,
That the race from dust created
  Might not perish utterly,
Which the dreadful Law had sentenced
  In the depths of hell to lie,

O how blest that wondrous birthday,
  When the Maid the curse retrieved,
Brought to birth mankind's salvation,
  By the Holy Ghost conceived;
And the Babe, the world's Redeemer,
  In her loving arms received,

This is he, whom seer and sybil
  Sang in ages long gone by;
This is he of old revealèd
  In the page of prophecy;
Lo! he comes, the promised Saviour;
  Let the world his praises cry!

Sing, ye heights of heaven, his praises;
  Angels and Archangels, sing!
Wheresoe'er ye be, ye faithful,
  Let your joyous anthems ring,
Every tongue his name confessing,
  Countless voices answering,

Hail! thou Judge of souls departed;
  Hail! of all the living King!
On the Father's right hand thronèd,
  Through his courts thy praises ring,
Till at last for all offences
  Righteous judgement thou shalt bring,

Now let old and young uniting
   Chant to thee harmonious lays,
Maid and matron hymn thy glory,
   Infant lips their anthem raise,
Boys and girls together singing
   With pure heart their song of praise,

Let the storm and summer sunshine,
   Gliding stream and sounding shore,
Sea and forest, frost and zephyr,
   Day and night their Lord adore;
Let creation join to laud thee
   Through the ages evermore (EH. 613).

10

A grotesque children's hymn by Mrs. C. F. Alexander which is in a widely
used hymnbook (see p. 78).

Within the churchyard, side by side,
   Are many long low graves;
And some have stones set over them,
   On some the green grass waves.

Full many a little Christian child,
   Woman, and man, lies there;
And we pass near them every time
   When we go in to prayer.

They cannot hear our footsteps come,
   They do not see us pass;
They cannot feel the warm bright sun
   That shines upon the grass.

They do not hear when the great bell
   Is ringing overhead;
They cannot rise and come to Church
   With us, for they are dead.

But we believe a day shall come
   When all the dead will rise,
When they who sleep down in the grave
   Will ope again their eyes.

For Christ our Lord was buried once,
   He died and rose again,

He conquer'd death, He left the grave;
And so will Christian men.

So when the friends we love the best
Lie in their churchyard bed,
We must not cry too bitterly
Over the happy dead;

Because, for our dear SAVIOUR's sake,
Our sins are all forgiven;
And Christians only fall asleep
To wake again in Heav'n (HAMSt. 575).

11

A children's hymn by G. W. Briggs (see p. 79).

God my Father, loving me,
Gave his Son, my friend to be:
Gave his Son, my form to take,
Bearing all things for my sake.

Jesus still remains the same
As in days of old he came;
As my brother by my side,
Still he seeks my steps to guide.

How can I repay thy love,
Lord of all the hosts above?
What have I, a child, to bring
Unto thee, thou heavenly King?

I have but myself to give:
Let me to thy glory live;
Let me follow, day by day,
Where thou showest me the way (SP. 357).

12

A children's hymn, by Lesbia Scott, using contemporary language; as given in *The BBC Hymn Book* and *The Hymnal 1940* (see p. 79).

I sing a song of the saints of God,
Patient and brave and true,

Who toiled and fought and lived and died
 For the Lord they loved and knew.
And one was a doctor, and one was a queen,
And one was a shepherdess on the green:
They were all of them saints of God; and I mean,
 God helping, to be one too.

They loved their Lord so dear, so dear,
 And his love made them strong;
And they followed the right, for Jesus' sake,
 The whole of their good lives long.
And one was a soldier and one was a priest,
And one was slain by a fierce wild beast:
And there's not any reason, no, not the least,
 Why I shouldn't be one too.

They lived not only in ages past,
 There are hundreds of thousands still;
The world is bright with the joyous saints
 Who love to do Jesus' will.
You can meet them in school, or in lanes, or at sea,
In church, or in trains, or in shops, or at tea,
For the saints of God are just folk like me,
 And I mean to be one too (H. 243, BBC. 353).

13

Part of a hymn for missions, by James Montgomery (see p. 89).

Lift up your heads, ye gates of brass;
 Ye bars of iron, yield,
And let the King of glory pass:
 The Cross is in the field.

That banner, brighter than the star
 That leads the train of night,
Shines on their march, and guides from far
 His servants to the fight.

A holy war those servants wage;
 Mysteriously at strife,
The powers of heaven and hell engage
 For more than death or life.

Ye armies of the living God,
 His sacramental host!

Where hallowed footsteps never trod,
　　Take your appointed post.

Though few and small and weak your bands,
　　Strong in your Captain's strength,
Go to the conquest of all lands,
　　All must be his at length.

Uplifted are the gates of brass,
　　The bars of iron yield;
Behold the King of glory pass;
　　The Cross hath won the field (EH. 549).

14

This is an example of Scripture mishandled in a hymn. It was written by Mrs. L. M. Willis in 1864 and is very popular in England (see p. 101).

Father, hear the prayer we offer;
　　Not for ease that prayer shall be,
But for strength that we may ever
　　Live our lives courageously.

Not for ever in green pastures
　　Do we ask our way to be;
But the steep and rugged pathway
　　May we tread rejoicingly.

Not for ever by still waters
　　Would we idly rest and stay;
But would smite the living fountains
　　From the rocks along our way.

Be our strength in hours of weakness,
　　In our wanderings be our Guide;
Through endeavour, failure, danger,
　　Father, be thou at our side (EH. 385).

15

Reginald Heber at his most romantic. This hymn is still very popular in Scotland, and much sung, both at baptisms and funerals (see p. 104).

By cool Siloam's shady rill
　　How sweet the lily grows!

How sweet the breath, beneath the hill
    Of Sharon's dewy rose!

Lo! such the child whose early feet
    The paths of peace have trod,
Whose secret heart, with influence sweet
    Is upward drawn to God.

By cool Siloam's shady rill
    The lily must decay;
The rose that blooms beneath the hill
    Must shortly fade away.

And soon, so soon, the wintry hour
    Of man's maturer age
Will shake the soul with sorrow's power,
    And stormy passion's rage!

O Thou, whose infant feet were found
    Within Thy Father's shrine,
Whose years, with changeless virtue crowned,
    Were all alike divine,

Dependent on Thy bounteous breath,
    We seek Thy grace alone,
In childhood, manhood, age, and death,
    To keep us still Thine own (CH. 309, vss. 3-4 omitted).

16

Reginald Heber at his best (see p. 105).

I praised the earth, in beauty seen,
With garlands gay of various green;
I praised the sea, whose ample field
Shone glorious as a silver shield;
And earth and ocean seemed to say,
"Our beauties are but for a day."

I praised the sun, whose chariot rolled
On wheels of amber and of gold;
I praised the moon, whose softer eye
Gleamed sweetly through the summer sky;
And moon and sun in answer said,
"Our days of light are numbered."

O God, O good beyond compare,
If thus thy meaner works are fair,
If thus thy beauties gild the span
Of ruined earth and sinful man,
How glorious must the mansion be
Where thy redeemed shall dwell with thee (SP. 533).

17

Part of a hymn by Augustus M. Toplady, which because of its original
first verse has fallen into unmerited disuse. The original is in sixteen verses,
of which seven appear in the *Church Hymnary*, beginning with Toplady's
opening line, "Your harps, ye trembling saints, Down from the willows take."
Verses 4-7 of the *Church Hymnary's* version follow here, which are verses 7, 8, 13,
and 16 of the original (see p. 124).

When we in darkness walk,
Nor feel the heavenly flame,
Then is the time to trust our God
And rest upon His Name.

Soon shall our doubts and fears
Subside at His control,
His loving-kindness shall break through
The midnight of the soul.

Wait till the shadows flee;
Wait thy appointed hour;
Wait till the Bridegroom of thy soul
Reveals His love with power.

Blest is the man, O God,
That stays himself on Thee:
Who wait for Thy salvation, Lord,
Shall Thy salvation see (CH. 561).

18

A hymn of personal vocation by Charles Wesley. The first five verses appear
in *The Methodist Hymn-Book;* verses 1, 3, 4, and 5 in the 1877 edition of *A
Collection of Hymns for the Use of the People Called Methodists;* and verses
1, 4, and 5 only, in the 1780 edition of that collection. Verse 6 has never been
used in a Methodist hymnal. The hymn is unusual, therefore, in having been
treated with increasing respect by Methodists as the years have passed (see
p. 152).

Servant of all, to toil for man
Thou didst not, Lord, refuse;
Thy majesty did not disdain
To be employed for us.

Son of the carpenter, receive
This humble work of mine;
Worth to my meanest labour give,
By joining it to Thine.

End of my every action Thou,
In all things Thee I see;
Accept my hallowed labour now,
I do it unto Thee.

Thy bright example I pursue,
To Thee in all things rise;
And all I think, or speak, or do
Is one great sacrifice.

Careless through outward cares I go,
From all distraction free;
My hands are but engaged below,
My heart is still with Thee (MHB. 575).

O, when wilt Thou, my Life, appear!
How gladly will I cry,
"Tis done, the work Thou gav'st me here,
"Tis finished, Lord!"—and die! [1]

---

[1] *The Poetical Works of John and Charles Wesley*, arranged by G. Osborn (London: Wesleyan-Methodist Conference Office, 1868), I, 172.

Appendix C

Index of First Lines of Hymns Discussed in This Book with Chart Showing Their Appearance in Various Hymnals

The abbreviations used in the chart on the following pages are given on page 7. An X in the column M indicates that the hymn is to be in the forthcoming revision of the Methodist Hymnal. Parentheses around a number indicate a variation in the first line. Where no reference to other appearances is found in this index, a full reference is given in the text where the hymn is mentioned.

	L	CS	PR	M	OA	CU	CE	EH	SP	MHB	CP
A charge to keep I have, 105, 149			301	287/X		362				578	
Abide with me, 115	576		64	520/X	26	550	16	363	437	948	622
According to thy gracious word, 115	266	133	444	410/X		227	227	300	259	763	301
All creatures of our God, 148	173	16	100	65/X	86	29	399		439	28	31
All praise to thee, my God, 144	223		63	51/X	28	544	20	(267)	(45)	(943)	(617)
All under the leaves, 64											
All ye who know that, 157											
Almighty Father of all things, 148				/X							461
And have the bright immensities, 54, 152											
At even when the sun was set, 144, 150	232		55	48/X	30	541	19	266	42	689	63?
At the cross her station, 64	84			138/	341		145	115	185	185	
At the Lamb's high feast, 62	95						161	128			
Awake, my soul, 143, 149	202	4		34/X	6	529	2	257	25	931	590
Be thou my vision, 150		194	303	/X		336	568			632	432
Breathe on me, Breath of God, 34	470		235	180/X	141	148	485		458	300	216
Brightest and best, 105	53	66	175	119/X	338	49	356	41	85	122	94
Captain of Israel's host, 105						440			462	608	496
Can you count the stars, 79				/X							

	L	CS	PR	M	OA	CU	CE	EH	SP	MHB	CP
Christ rides to the holy war, 82.	208										
Christ whose glory fills, 143.		1	47	32/X	7	535	5	258	26	924	594
Christians, awake, 74.	19			93/		67	78	21	73	120	83
Christians, to the Paschal, 58.								130			
City of God, 84.	330	249	436	420/		171	624	375	468	703	253
Close by the heedless worker's, 152.									469		
Come, Holy Ghost, our hearts, 34.				175/X		155				305	226
Come, let us remember, 83.											
Come, let us to the Lord, 149.	471		125			269	118			342	386
Come, O thou Traveller, 25, 40, 44.	5			311/X		312		378	476	339	495
Come, thou long-expected, 151.	106	39	151	84/X		132	548	131		242	159
Come, ye faithful, 57.		102	205	151/X	360		165		144		140
Come, ye thankful people, 126.	363	32	525	545/X	65	577	307	289	9	962	645
Eternal beam of light divine, 113.					145	417				496	395
Eternal Father, strong to save, 27.	338	236	521	553/X		452	301	540	336	917	680
Eternal light, 35, 149.			486			36				544	21
Father eternal, Ruler of, 95, 103, 115.		330		/X					326		
Father, hear the prayer, 27, 98.							454	385	487		523

	L	CS	PR	M	OA	CU	CE	EH	SP	MHB	CP
Father of Jesus Christ, 26				203/						561	475
Forever here my rest shall be, 100				373/						456	
Forth in thy Name, O Lord, 143, 149	214	313		290/X	13	350	7	259	29	590	593
Forth rode the knights of old, 82					342					819	533
Forty days and forty nights, 152		70					105	73	97	165	
From all that dwell below, 121, 150	429		33	17/X		16	352		408	4	746
Gentle Christ, 170											
Glorious things of thee, 30	152	279	434	382/X	97	166	618	393	500	706	243
Go it alone, 171											
God my Father, loving me, 77, 185									357	840	689
God of grace and God of glory, 95		319	358	279/X							563
Guide me, O thou great Jehovah, 115, 149	520	235	339	301/X		441	406	397	508	615	500
Hail the day that sees him, 52, 177	111	107	146			114	174	143	172	221	154
Hail to the Lord's Anointed, 151	328	36		85/X		139	396	45	87	245	326
Hark, the glad sound, 151	6				313	54	65	6	62	82	74
Hark! the herald angels sing, 74, 112	25	50	163	86/X	326	59	77	24	74	117	84
Holy, Holy, Holy, 104, 153	131	168	11	1/X	16	1	1	162	187	36	223
Holy eternal Son of God, 167											

	L	CS	PR	M	OA	CU	CE	EH	SP	MHB	CP
Hosanna to the living Lord, 105..........	424										
I bind unto myself today, 55, 177..........		170					812	212	528	392	753
I danced in the morning, 169..........											
I know a rose-tree springing, (73)									533		
I praised the earth, 105, 188..........											
I sing a song of the saints, 79, 185..........											
I would choose to be a door-keeper, 167 ...									196		
Immortal, invisible, 150..........	172	113	85	64/X	103	34	401	407	535	34	28
In the bleak mid-Winter, 73..........	36	53		104/X		56	691	25	75	137	90
It came upon the midnight, 74.	23		160	92/X	327	58	319	26	76	130	88
It is finished! Christ hath, 67..........								118	139		
Jesus, good above all other, 79..........								598	540		464
Jesus lives, 57..........					361	116	606	134	155	216	147
Jesus, lover of my soul, 31..........	393		216	338/X	192	266	510	414	542	110	473
Jesus, tender Shepherd, 29..........	235			452/		622	696	599	364	844	703
Jesus, whose all-redeeming, 158..........											
Judge eternal, 95..........	343	261	517	/X	300	515	659	423	552	883	572
King of glory, 150..........					106		803	424	553	23	426

	L	CS	PR	M	OA	CU	CE	EH	SP	MHB	CP
Lamp of our feet, 123			254	/X							229
Let all the world in, 150	418	136	22	8/X	108	38		427	556	5	3
Let saints on earth, 89				422/X	277	(176)	611	428	557	(824)	(361)
Let us thank the Christ, 85											
Lift up your heads, ye gates, 89	308					260	387	549	301	265	324
Lo! he comes, 144	13	44	234	/X		136	60	7	65	264	160
Lord Christ, when first, 96, 127		157		/X					562	906	172
Lord, my weak thought in vain, 148					229				563		
Lord of all being, 150	170	112	87	62/X	110	20	421	434	564	32	23
Lord of our life, and God, 25	157	215				165	470	435	349	729	508
Love divine, all loves, 45, 104, 121, 153	397	206	399	372/X	166	330		437	573	431	179
Loving shepherd of thy sheep, 29							698	602			
Mine eyes have seen the glory, 123	356			/X	298		335		578	260	170
My God, how wonderful thou art, 26, 149	181				114	18	370	441	581	73	24
My Shepherd will supply my need, 28, 175		228									50
My soul, there is a country, 159					285				585	466	356
Nature with open volume, 68, 160-61											129
Now thank we all our God, 127, 150	443	237	9	7/X	116	19	305	533	350	10	42

	L	CS	PR	M	OA	CU	CE	EH	SP	MHB	CP
Now the day is over, 144.	231		51	53/X	41	545	42	603	49	944	627
O come, all ye faithful, 73.	42	46	170	96/X		47	75	28	78	118	85
O come and mourn with me, 65.	86		192	134/		90	141	111	140	187	135
O come, O come, Emmanuel, 144, 151.	2	34	147	83/X	315	137	62	8	66	257	72
O for a thousand tongues, 62.	428		141	162/X		41	377	446	595	1	180
O gladsome light, 144.	220	13	61		42	551	34	269	50	936	611
O God of Bethel, 149.	519	214	342			446	429	447	596	607	55
O God of earth and altar, 91-93.	344	260	511	/X				562	308		578
O God of truth, 149.		71				411	553	449	597		522
O holy city, seen of John, 96.		264	508	474/X		382					
O Lord of hosts, all heaven, 148.		348						458	606		
O love, how deep, how broad, 152.							475	459		62	63
O man, what troubled thoughts, 85.											
O Master Workman of the race, 121, 152.			178	118/X			647				
O sons and daughters, 58.	96	100	206	/X	362	106	162	(626)	(143)		724
O Thou who camest from above, 105.		207		344/X		344		343	256	386	438
Of the Father's heart, 26, 74, 183.	17	48	7	/X	330	52	79	613	387	83	76
On Jordan's bank, 152.	4	37					67	9	67		73

	L	CS	PR	M	OA	CU	CE	EH	SP	MHB	CP
Once in royal David's city, 77	41		462	442/		70	733	605	368	859	89
Once to every man and nation, 103	547	270	361	263/X	306	410	651	563	309	898	388
One who is all unfit to count, 151	384					279	527			159	388
Onward, Christian soldiers, 87	560		350	280/X	250	401	412	643	397	822	527
Our blest Redeemer, 34				177/	130	162	489	157	182	283	209
Praise, my soul, 149	160	127	31	77/X		17	353	470	623	12	18
Praise to the Holiest, 149	411					14	384	471	625	74	71
Praise to the Lord, 150	408	132	1	60/X	131	9	393	536	626	64	45
Remember all the people, 79	317		495						369	864	344
Ride on! ride on in majesty, 65, 104	73	78	188	125/X	355	85	131	620	137	192	122
Rise up, O men of God, 121	541	310	352	267/X	256	378	656		635	585	561
See the conqueror mounts, 56	112						176	145	173	223	
Shepherd divine, our wants, 45							442		118	736	494
Sing, my tongue, the glorious, 64, 181	61					129	129	95	129		125
Soldiers of Christ, arise, 87	564	328	362	282/X	251	404	419	479	641	484	497
Sometimes a light surprises, 149	495		418	351/X	221	287			643	527	398
Son of God, eternal Saviour, 95	542	305						529	339		558
Son of the carpenter, 152, 190										(575)	

	L	CS	PR	M	OA	CU	CE	EH	SP	MHB	CP
Songs of praise the angels, 115	432						391	481	644		15
Sun of my soul, 144	226	210	56	56/X	45	556	18	274	55	942	621
Teach me, my God and King, 149, 159	451			320/X	183			485	652	597	433
The Church's one foundation, 39	149	172	437	381/X	258	164	563	489	249	701	254
The day of Resurrection, 57	105	96	208	159/X	365	103	164	137	146	208	141
The day Thou gavest, 144	227	15	59	54/X	52	568	27	277	56	667	626
The duteous day now closeth, 144, 148	228	17						278	57		629
The God of Abraham praise, 62, 110, 153	410		89	5/X	132	25	371	646	398	21	12
The God of love my shepherd, 28					232			93	653	51	43
The head that once was, 54	439		211	163/X	371	118	590	147	175	244	164
The King of love, 29	530	230	106	353/X	203	280	539	490	654	76	61
The Lord is rich and merciful, 151											370
The Lord will come, 121	327	251	230	/X			64	492	658	813	156
The Lord's my Shepherd, 150	522	229	104	70/X	126	637	547			50	729
The royal banners forward go, 64, 181	75	82			(340)		128	94	130	184	126
The spacious firmament, 148	442	345	97	66/X	72	27	602	297	659	44	30
The sun is sinking fast, 144					51		21	280		939	614
The whole bright world, 57									167		

	L	CS	PR	M	OA	CU	CE	EH	SP	MHB	CP
There is a green hill, 65	77		202	135/X		87	545	106	131	180	136
There is a land of pure, 40	583			528/		464	620	498	201	649	359
Thou art the Way, 152	390		221	332/X		339	591			160	102
Thou hidden Love of God, 149	391			375/X	204	307			671	433	469
Thy ceaseless, unexhausted, 150						12				49	
To God with heart, 55									176		151
To-morrow shall be my dancing, 165, 179											
Triumphant Zion, lift, 149											319
Wake, awake, for night, 36, 123	7	43			318	134		12	687	255	(760)
We thank you, Lord of heaven, 81									692		
"Welcome, happy morning!", 57	93		207	161/X	367	107	168			212	139
We're told of one whose eyes, 83											
When a knight won his spurs, 81									377		535
When all thy mercies, 46, 150	440		119	542/X	22	23	381	511	694	413	49
When I survey, 69, 96, 160	503	90	198	148/X	353	86	593	107	133	182	131
When we in darkness walk, 123											(401)
Where cross the crowded ways, 92	351	265	507	465/X	271	380	654			895	
Who is this with garments gory, 65								108			

	L	CS	PR	M	OA	CU	CE	EH	SP	MHB	CP
With joy we meditate, 152						125				236	97
Ye fair green hills, 152				124/		84					106
Ye watchers and ye holy ones, 153	437	240	34	6/X			398	519			
Your harps, ye trembling, 189											

Index of Names
and Subjects